About the Publisher - Mentor Masters

Mentor Masters Ltd is a leading professional coaching, consulting, training and business content provider. The owners have many years' experience in leading businesses across multiple sectors. The company provides executive coaching services for business leaders and new managers, focusing on leadership, growth and personal development. Our aim is to consult on business plans, business strategy and improvement programmes. We run in-house training on Lean Six Sigma, sales pipeline and sales motivation training. Mentor Masters have supported many businesses in achieving their long-term financial objectives and exit strategies.

As a content provider, we create business, leadership, coaching and change books; ranging from personal development programs, through to full coaching manuals. Visit our website or the Amazon store for more details.

About the Author - Martin Lacey

Martin Lacey is the Founder of B2C App start-up Compete Impossible, the first all-in-one performance app for athletes and professionals. Including activity tracking, leagues, and live in-person or virtual race events, power by a global rewards marketplace.

He previously was a shareholder and company director for an international consulting business for over 6 years. During this time, he advised many hyper-growth technology companies on best practice around building their businesses at scale Internationally. Martin, with his business partners, grew their organisation from a small company with one local office to a global brand with multiple offices located in Dubai, Singapore and London with 80+ staff by the end of 2019.

Martin is a passionate hands-on leader who values integrity and a focus on emotional intelligence to put people and customers first. He has over 10 years' experience in leading teams and consulting with technology companies.

Climb Your Everest with Everyone

Leader & Management Handbook

Martin Lacey

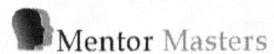Mentor Masters

Content Page

Introduction   11
Chapter 1   Have you Chosen Leadership   22
             or has it Chosen You?
1.1   What is the Role of a   22
             Manager and Leader?
1.2   Common Personality Types   27
1.3   How does a Manager and   37
             Leader Make You Feel?

Chapter 2   Leader's Vision and Values   43
2.1   Vision   45
2.2   Values   49
2.3   Building Pride in the Group   51

Chapter 3   The We, the Me and the   58
             Victim
3.1   Staff Facts   58
3.2   The Importance of   62
             Accountability
3.3   Favouritism and Top People   68
3.4   No Two People are the Same   75
3.5   Motivation   82
3.6   Hiring   86
3.7   Firing   95

Chapter 4	Leadership Formula	100
4.1	Trust	100
4.2	Personal Communication and Engagement	103
4.3	Importance of Delegation	105
4.4	Managing Change	107
4.5	Asking Good Questions	113
4.6	Coaching and Feedback	117
Chapter 5	Mirror Management	124
5.1	The Skill of Managing Yourself	124
5.2	Types of Decisions	128
Chapter 6	Accepting Failure and Disappointment	132
6.1	Difficult Roads Often Lead to Beautiful Destinations	132
6.2	Organisation Environment	135
6.3	The Great Leaver	136
6.4	The Comeback is More Important than the Setback	138
Chapter 7	Choosing and Managing the Boss	142
7.1	Managers to Avoid	143
7.2	Understanding Your Manager	144
7.3	Rules for Managing the Boss	147

Chapter 8	Value & Due Diligence	151
8.1	Personal Value	151
8.2	Understanding Your Value	154
8.3	How to Increase Your Personal Value	156
8.4	Due Diligence	157
8.5	Types of Companies	160
Chapter 9	Winning Success and Happiness	165
9.1	Winning Mentality	165
9.2	Positive Mental Attitude	167
9.3	Power of Expectation	168
9.4	Emotionally Fit	169
9.5	Successful Culture	170
Chapter 10	Reaching the Summit	173
10.1	Own It	174
10.2	Goals & Dreams	175
10.3	Think Big	176
10.4	The Master of What You Choose	176
10.5	The Power of Courage	177
10.6	Find the Positives in People	178
10.7	Don't be Governed by Fear	179
10.8	The Importance of Time	180
10.9	Validation	180

10.10	Live in Reality	181
10.11	Learn from Experience	182
10.12	Power of Mindfulness	183
Conclusion	Build your Own Narrative	185
	Acknowledgements	187

Climb Your Everest with Everyone

Leader & Management Handbook

Martin Lacey

Introduction

"An opportunity is what you make of it."
Martin Lacey

If someone asked you tomorrow to climb Everest, you would think they were crazy, right? You're totally unprepared, have self-limiting beliefs, and don't have the core skills or confidence to achieve it. However, with the correct leadership over a month, could it be done? Could a great leader convince you that it can be done, train you on the task and then execute it? I am a firm believer that great leadership inspires people and moves them to achieve things they could have never done before. This is being proven every day in 2020.

Covid-19 has a grip on the Earth's health and economy. We have moved into a quick and unexpected recession. Leaders are all coping with loss, disappointment and frustration over something that they could not have controlled. This is having a large impact on their businesses and their people. Yet, we are seeing individual and team pieces of bravery, brilliance and leadership surround us. This ranges from NHS staff and front-line workers, to communities coming together to support each other through a difficult time. This year more than ever, we have seen that hard-working, focused teams can achieve brilliant goals; especially in the face of adversity and a common objective. This book is based around empowering you to feel that you can lead your staff or business to perform better and reach brilliance. We will focus on how people feel being led, how they connect to you and how you build lifelong relationships. I call it the "leadership flex" - which is leadership based on context and circumstance. The ability to get a good result and make the right decision despite a challenging situation. No two moments are ever the exact same in life, and as a leader you have to flex in between styles based on the situation. Your staff will feel through working with you that together, you can achieve your Everest - whatever that might be.

This book is for managers looking for a path into improved leadership. This could be those early in their career who are looking for guidance on how to lead and make their teams excel. It will show you how to drive a sense of empowerment, build a strong cohesive unit and become more self-confident. The context and advice given in this book can be used across industry and across many aspects of a business, including technology sales, estate agents, manufacturing teams, recruitment teams or even for CEOs/MDs/ founders. Leadership skills and practises are fundamentally the same across any group, and throughout this book we will focus as much as possible on a broad context.

I want to start by briefly telling you my story and experience in leadership, and what inspired me to create this book. From 2010 to 2020, I worked for an international recruitment and consulting business in the UK, specialising in Technology with a global footprint. I earned over six figures from 23-years-old, and was made a shareholder at 24-years-old. This meant running a one-million-pound business unit with no management or leadership training. I have been lucky enough to not only experience personally scaling a business, but I also worked with some of the most disruptive technology companies on the planet, and their executives, in building high performing teams. I had key roles in defining culture, process, business plans and running the profit/loss. Most importantly, I had the privilege of interviewing hundreds of technology professionals and sales leaders from all over the US, Europe and Asia. This included partnering with

CEOs from Silicon Valley and some of the very best venture capitalists.

During this time, I read many management and sports leadership books. Frankly, most were excellent and I was always able to take something away from them. However, something always bugged me. This became clearer the more leaders I personally interviewed and the more teams I managed directly. Generally, most books were focused around case studies of elite teams or business, such as Manchester United Football Club, SAS, Navy Seals, Apple, Harvard University or an NBA basketball team. When the reality of day to day leadership for most of us is that we are working within constraints and under a totally unique circumstance. Our teams are motivated, but not trained SAS commandos, Apple's elite development team or Olympic athletes. We don't have an unlimited budget, coaching staff or fans screaming our names after every call and are not paid millions every year. We are squeezing every drop out of what we have available to us. The people that are sitting in front of us every day are good honest employees who are looking to take their careers and lives forward, mostly entrusting that responsibility on us and our business. Often, the role of a leader is to get the best out of what you have and find a way to bring people together to reach a common goal. This is built on trust, relationships, inspiration, coaching and often, firefighting during real life situations as they unfold.

I personally grew up in a small town south of Birmingham in the UK. My father came from a working-class background in Leicester and went on to obtain a Chemistry degree from Norwich, and has had a successful 30-year career in business. He was the MD of a business and led a successful management buyout that secured his financial future. My Mum was from South London, her parents were both doctors. She went on to study Biology, and became a Biology teacher for 30 years at a school in Birmingham. I am absolutely positive that she has inspired a generation of scientists and doctors we see today. My parents were fun, organised, hardworking, and valued education and competition throughout my upbringing. They encouraged me and my sister to follow every opportunity, take every chance.

Growing up I was an extremely average student and at around 11-years-old I was also diagnosed with dyslexia. By the age of 15, most teachers had given up on my prospects of having any kind of success in either my life or career. I remember meeting with a career's counsellor once, at around age 14. At the time, I wanted to be in business or be a marine biologist – they actually laughed and told me to be more realistic. The fact is, they were right too. I always left studying too late or did not feel motivated to do so, but as a teenager, I had a wake-up call. I managed to prepare for my GCSE's in around 6 weeks, giving me the push to get 9 GCSEs at a decent standard.

I followed this with A Levels and a Bachelor of Science with Honours in Sport Development with Coaching from Sheffield Hallam University. Throughout my life, I competed at every sport imaginable and often to a very high level, especially football, athletics and swimming. I was often selected for sports teams I had never actually played, such as cricket and rugby. In fact, I turned up to our school cricket game in shorts once; everyone else was wearing cricket whites. I stood out in the field and made a catch, went in to bat and smashed the ball a few times. I loved team sports and any activity which was based on physical or mental battles. Through my degree, I was also given the chance to coach sports teams at a variety of different levels, and to work with a diverse group of young people.

I believed all of my experiences were transferable to a career in business, sales and leadership. The truth is, I always felt a burning inside me to achieve something more. Throughout my childhood and teens, I often felt I had given up too soon with certain things, and this is something I only understood later. I had goals and objectives replaying in my head from an early age. I remember visiting Bath as a child and seeing the huge four-story houses and thinking to myself, "I want a five-bedroom house before I'm 30." At that age I didn't know how I was going to do it, but it happened.

I always want to win and work extremely hard to do so. I fundamentally believe you have to out-work your competition before anything else strategic can happen. When I joined my first recruitment company, I was lucky enough to sit near the top biller. There were two in the office at the time. My first principle was to see the hours he worked; see his output and organisation, and then work harder than him. I used to arrive 15 minutes before him and leave 15 minutes after him every day. I did this for three years. I am also a firm believer that it is what people do outside the office when no one is watching, that matters more. I spent hours watching videos on technology and different businesses, studying for my own CISSP exam and downloading whitepapers on our clients at weekends and evenings. This meant my time on the phone was sharper; I understood technology better and my conversations with customers improved. Needless to say, from joining as a trainee, after two years I had become the highest biller, then best divisional manager, then company director after just four years of employment.

For the next 6 years we focused on building our SME. At the start, we had around 12 people in one UK office in the Midlands. The following years we opened in Singapore, Dubai and London. We grew to around 80 staff at our largest and released many new successful service lines. By the end of 2019, we had become truly recognized as a leader in our field and quadrupled our enterprise valuation. We did it the hard way, never taking VC funding or financial help during this time. I can tell you honestly, working and running a recruitment agency, you start to see it all. From your own staff, to your clients and candidates, people show all sides of human behaviour. One day can be so high, and the next so low. Leading people in a totally unpredictable environment is difficult and I believe it is one of the most difficult sales leadership jobs you can have. You're often working with young people who have not had much or any success yet and are searching for instant gratification. Teaching patience and GRIT causes huge challenges.

Imagine a leader with a large sales team during an uncertain world. You are three or four layers away from where you can make money in a high-pressure growth cooker. It is volatile, uncertain, complex and ambiguous, with events changing sometimes hourly or daily. I absolutely loved it. This means that the ownership or accountability of success is very easy to avoid for the staff; they can simply find a customer to blame for them not achieving, and to be honest, they were sometimes right. Managing in this environment, you have to build real relationships with the people who work for you. You need to react quickly to coach and build loyalty if you ever want to get a result.

During my personal years in sales leadership, I built many teams. The smallest being a "tiger team" which was a group of three, and the largest of around fifteen within a specific technology vertical. These were built from absolute scratch with no customers, no strong branding, little training, a competitive market and working to a low budget. It was fun and empowering. I have no doubt that great leadership can empower people to become anything – I have seen it first-hand.

Nevertheless, I want to be clear, I have had failure and success in both parts. The losses are what you learn from. All the highly successful leaders I have interviewed have told me that they have been sacked at least once due to performance or because teams did not achieve targets. It happens. Pushing yourself outside of your comfort zone means you will often meet success and failure in equal measures. No successful person prepares for failure, so it can feel alien or destructive. It's a lonely place, but more about that later.

Success in leadership is a marathon not a sprint, and in this book we will cover a large element of becoming successful in leadership, always keeping in mind that leadership is extremely contextual and the groups we manage are diverse.

Finally, before you start, I want to say that I am not and have not been the perfect leader or manager. I have not met or worked with a leader in technology in eleven years who would claim to be the ideal leader. Most leaders divide opinions, but aim to change people's lives for the good. They are, however, always blamed and accountable for the bad as well.

As a leader you have to always be you - don't settle for something that you are not happy with. It is very difficult for a leader to mould into a group, but easy for a group to change for a leader, and not everyone is always going to follow you. Most people will though, if you have energy, knowledge, vision and you value them. Be you, you're doing okay, and don't give up too soon. Hopefully, through this book you can learn the leadership flex.

Chapter 1: Have You Chosen Leadership or has it Chosen You?

"Leadership is unlocking people's potential to become better." Bill Bradley

1.1 What is the Role of the Manager and a Leader?

You're a manager – great! Now what? How did you get here? I am going to make some sensible assumptions before we get started. Firstly, you're extremely competent at your role as an individual so you have the basic skills to teach others. You could have been selected for the role externally and gone through a long interview process to join the company. You could have recently been promoted through longevity, success and loyalty. As a result, you now have your own new sub-team to run. Or this could be the second or third time managing a group and you want to do better than last time. You're looking for a fresh perspective. As you can see, you can take a managerial role for many different reasons and it is important to understand, why? The why factor becomes more important as time goes on and you are tested within your position.

There's also the reality that it could be a group you did not select to manage and you have no resources to hire new people. You could also be building a team from scratch and are about to start hiring for the first time, setting the foundations for success. Let's be totally honest, you could be happy or unhappy with the group you have today, but you are going to have to learn quickly how to get a response out of them. You will need to make the best of the team that you have, or bring in new blood if you can. During this first chapter, we are going to look at what a manager/leader actually is, and the different types of personalities you tend to find.

In the role you have undertaken, I am assuming you will need both management and leadership skills. Most upper to middle management roles require both skills. So it is important to understand at a high level, what a manager and leader actually do. It is important that you recognise the difference and when to use each. To be a successful performer in your role, you need to understand that management and leadership is a balance. This could be the difference between leadership vs. management time in a week, or when to take control and when to delegate across your team. Finding the balance in emotion across a week is an important part – for example be authoritative in the Monday morning meeting to set standards, but more open and friendly at lunch time. Balance, consistency and discipline should be your best friend day to day. The main tasks will usually include-

- **Setting Standards;** your first priority is setting standards. This means having accountability and responsibility for targets and goals. You must have clear expectations of the values and behaviours of the team, and hold individuals accountable to the standards you have set.
- **Planning and Organising;** ensuring that your people and resources are effectively utilised to get the work done. Making sure that you delegate tasks where appropriate, whilst maintaining control to deliver on time and well.
- **Monitoring and Controlling Activity;** focusing on measuring and tracking progress. Making sure that you understand when to intervene and when to take action to ensure that goals and targets are delivered.
- **Communicating;** strong focus on communication and making sure you do so clearly, often and when necessary. Making

sure to understand when to adjust the style for the team or individual.

- **Developing Teamwork;** making sure that you have clear expectations of the team, motivate the team to work together and strive for a bigger goal. Foster an atmosphere of open communication, and create a collaborative environment at all times.
- **Managing People and Performance;** it is important to build relationships, trust and have empathy with staff. This includes coaching and providing feedback. Show support where needed and drive targets. Have a focus on the performance of individuals, and the group as a whole.
- **Improving Processes;** within your role it is critical to take the time to master and understand processes. As a leader, you must continually assess how things are done and how they can be improved.
- **Leadership;** a focus on integrity, making good decisions and being consistent. Having a positive influence on people through energy and enthusiasm. You must have strong problem solving skills and be good at managing conflict.

The Leadership Flex

As explained, there is a huge variety of responsibilities connected to leadership and management. This is especially the case if you're in a versatile position and a changing environment. It is essential that you understand moving between management and leadership tasks based on the context. Most people tend to lean toward one model that suits them. This gives them limited flexibility and can make it difficult to react to circumstances. The key to having leadership flex, is to be able to quickly adapt to situations appropriately, understand what actions are needed and act with emotional intelligence. You will find you work with different types of managers throughout your career and work under different circumstances. It is good to think about what type of leader you want to be. How do you want to be remembered and what would you want people to say about you? Think about the best leader you have worked with. What are their best characteristics? Good leadership is often the ability to move between different tasks, circumstances and relationships, always creating a positive result. Mastering this is the leadership flex.

1.2 Common Personality Types

When you think about what type of leader you want to be, we need to look at the common types of managers and leaders that we see every day in the workplace. It is critical to remember that circumstance is key, and sometimes one leader can suit a situation much better than another, or vice versa. You need to recognise what type of leader you are in a situation if you want to improve and fully understand how to be flexible. It is also important to reflect on how you got to be a leader; what you have done to get there and where are the gaps in your ability? In general, there are six different manager profiles that we should reflect on. It's important to understand that people can change, including you. The reality is that sometimes we do not like what we see in the mirror. Always remember that you are in control of the type of leader you want to be, and you can choose your style appropriate to the context.

The Structural Organiser - this is a person who assumes a leadership role purely based on organisational structure. These types of managers are focused on the tasks in hand, and what should be done. These people are very focused on policy and process, tending to make black and white decisions. They often have strong analytical skills and make good choices with data. In general, however, they make decisions that do not fully consider people and their feelings.

Successful: When new staff have/are joining and need direct instructions to follow. They are generally good in times of peace, structure and calm. They can be good at execution of strategies as they do not often care about being liked or disliked. When reporting, projects and data are important and timeline critical. They are able to keep things on track, staying to budgets and needing a detailed focus.	Poor Performance: Due to internal or external factors, a change in mission has occurred. This may require increased motivation and strong people management skills. This person tends to struggle if there are many different personalities in the group or if goals and targets are situational instead of being fixed. They find unforeseen circumstances that arise, a challenge. They may be poor at managing conflict.

Good at: Setting Standards, Planning and Organising, Improving Processes.	Poor at: Communicating, Developing Teamwork, Managing People and Performance, Leadership.

Friendly Expert or "The Coach" - this person may often be promoted because they are an expert and experienced in a particular field. This means that they can train and supervise others effectively. They are often liked and respected by the team because of their thorough knowledge of key subjects and principles.

Successful: In the first 6-12 months in a role or a new team, where training is important and there are not many challenges from the group. This could be during the introduction of new products or services. They will be good at supporting and supervising	Poor Performance: When the task involves vision, goal setting and general execution of strategy. When dealing with challenging teams, very low performers and strong performers, this person may have

underperformers. They have strong communication skills and are good at managing the current task. They tend to have high empathy and gain good rapport with the team.	difficulties. They lack long term vision, motivation and struggle with complex problems.
Good At: Communicating, Developing Teamwork, Managing People and Performance.	Poor At: Planning and Organising, Improving Processes, Leadership.

Safe Pair Of Hands - Moral, Credible and High Integrity - this individual has been placed in a leadership role because they are credible, trustworthy and calm. They are frequently individuals who have been successful themselves and are able to maintain the status quo.

Successful: This person tends to lead by example. They understand processes and procedures and	Poor Performance: They may struggle to understand new systems. They may be unable to relate to others

are clear about what needs to be done. They have good relationships with the business and the individuals within it. They are able to identify issues and problems early, and can step in quickly to solve them.	leading to a lack of patience when coaching, and unrealistic expectations. This means they can be poor at delegation and struggle to motivate people.
Good At: Setting Standards, Planning and Organising, Monitoring and Controlling Activity.	Poor At: Communication, Developing Teamwork and Leadership.

Charismatic and Selfless - this person tends to be placed in a leadership role because of enthusiasm, drive, energy, humour, and an ability to empower others. They are strong at working with others and people naturally respect them. Usually inspirational and goal focused, but may break the rules to achieve success. They will want to understand the full context of a situation before making a decision. Being strong team players, they often eat last and put their own needs behind others to achieve the goal. They are very good at hitting a moving target as they understand the context.

Successful: During a time of extreme difficulty or intense competition, this individual will excel at driving change. They can lead a new focus which makes them able to challenge the group and move in a new direction. Generally, they are good at dealing with any conflict or issues that arise. They tend to be good at achieving the "big goal" at any cost, and are able to both create and manage top performers. Highly creative and action focused when you need	Poor Performance: If new processes need to be introduced, or at times of low activity, this person may struggle. If reporting and systems are important this person may have a lack of attention to detail. They may find it difficult to work with negative people or staff who are not open to improvement.

someone who thinks outside the box to solve problems.	
Good At: Communicating, Developing Teamwork, Managing People and Performance, Leadership	Poor At: Planning and Organising, Controlling Activity, Setting Standards and Monitoring.

The Hot Air Leader - these people are often full of confidence in themselves and are persuasive with their story; quick to answer questions and have reasons or excuses for poor results. They are the champions of bullshit. They don't care about the real truth of a situation or the long term consequences. They just live for the moment, to look and sound like they know what they are doing. These people are often in position for the short term. They hang around just long enough to get noticed and then move on.

Successful: If there are short term problems that need to	Poor Performance: These people lack the discipline and drive to

be answered and they are presenting a believable story.	deliver results for themselves or others. They tend to get exposed when consistently failing to deliver the required result.
Good At: Communicating	Poor At: Managing People's Performance, Improving Processes and Leadership

The "Me" Leader - this individual usually has a very strong and dominant personality. Autocratic in their style of leadership, so what they say goes. They tend to surround themselves with 'yes people' who will go along with their ideas. Generally, they are not interested in challenges or new ideas from their staff; it's mainly about status and power. Often, they don't care if it is the right or wrong decision for the business, but like to force ideas by driving results through fear and energy. They tend to trample over people and steal their good ideas, living in a bubble because people do not want to communicate the truth. They often spend long periods of time trying to fix the wrong problem. This means that they can live in a distorted virtual world which can often be different from reality.

Successful: If there is a time of crisis or difficulty. They can drive a business with strict processes, procedures and plans in place. They can be relied upon to achieve short-term results.	Poor Performance: These people tend to have an unrealistic big picture view because of their distorted view of what is achievable. These managers tend to be poor in a creative collaborative environment. Staff do not feel their ideas are valued, and fear the ever changing mood swings of the boss. Top performers tend to be stifled and held back from their full potential.
Good at: Setting Standards, Communicating,	Poor At: Managing People and Performance, Improving Processes, Developing

Monitoring and Controlling.	Teamwork.

When you read the different styles above, you will often start to see people you have worked with and maybe yourself screaming out of the page. It is important to understand where you, (so far), have made the right choices and where you may have gone wrong. The best leaders are often a mix of two or three of the above style, and flex between them based on situational context. What I can say is, if it is purely title and/or money you are after, you will not get your team to Everest. They may not even get on the plane to base camp with you. Remember, ego is the enemy of good leadership. You're going to find what's discussed in this book unnatural and challenging at times also. There has to be a bigger picture; the satisfaction of improving others to really excel in leadership. From what I have seen, leaders emerge from a group because of skill, energy, desire, expertise and ambition. People can feel them coming, and they want to ride the wave.

1.3 How does a Manager and Leader Make You Feel?

So let's start by focusing on what the difference is between a "manager" and a "leader", and how they make you feel. Remember, how your staff feel is the centre to all other emotions. We often create realities, remember something or react based on how we feel at the time. If they feel empowered, trusted, confident and part of a bigger picture, they will soon start performing better without any further training or pay rises. Your staff will all see you, the organisation, and situations that occur differently.

There are some fundamental differences in acting as a manager or a leader, mainly in the way they think, act and make team members feel. Understanding how your staff feel as you flex between both models is critical if you are to succeed.

Manager Focus

Action:	Feeling of Team:
Uses the stick to motivate.	Can feel threatened rather than inspired.

Can make black and white decisions.	Lack of understanding and emotional intelligence.
Depends on Authority of position.	Feel 'told and instructed', not engaged on the task.
Use's 'I.'	Team's contribution does not matter.
Task focused rather than team focused.	Feel like a cog in a wheel, not valued in the task.
Follows Rules.	Stifles creativity and ideas on how to change and improve.

The Monitor Manager.	No genuine connection or interest from team.

Leader Focus

Action:	Feeling of Team:
Leads with the reward.	Motivated, positive and engaged - driven to get the result.
Encourages and generates enthusiasm to deliver team goals.	Feel empowered.
Breaks the rules to achieve the result when necessary.	They feel obstacles and roadblocks are removed - success matters.
Focus on their people.	Valued.

Open communicator.	Trusted.
Uses 'We.'	Drives collaboration.
Coaches.	Invested in their future.

How Does a Leader Make You Feel?

A leader should make you feel strong, empowered, valued, coached and ready to climb Everest.

At this stage, I want you to stop and think about a leader you have worked with before, or if you cannot think of one- think about a great leader in Sport, Politics or Business. How do they make you feel? What did you feel when you worked with them? Do your staff feel like that with you? Could they one day? Challenge yourself to be honest; if all of your staff were asked about you tomorrow, what would they say?

Understand, no one is perfect and of course some people, due to culture or values, are just never going to work well together. But I want you to think how you want people to feel when they are managed by you. A good leader should have the ability to tap in to emotions quickly and create goose-bumps down their spine. It is important to understand that people's emotions drive behaviour.

Summary

- Your role as a manager/leader will usually include setting standards, planning, organising, monitoring and controlling activity, communicating, developing teamwork, managing people and performance, improving processes, and finally, leadership.
- Remember that flexing in between all of these skills is critical to your success.
- There are different management types found in leadership positions. Understanding these will help you determine your own style, and when to apply it.
- Create the right balance between model and behaviours, but keep consistency.
- Think about "feelings." How does your team feel in a situation? How can that be affected by you?
- Incorporating empathy and emotional understanding will create the longest lasting connections.
- What type of leader do you want to be?

Chapter 2: Leader's Vision and Values

"Leadership is the capacity to translate vision to reality". Warren Bennis

So what is your Everest, and how are your team going to get there?

To start at the beginning, every team needs an ultimate goal and everything you do as a leader whether that's the vision, mission and values you set, should underpin that. They should lead back to it. It should always be referred to, and when asked, they and you should remember it.

One of the first questions I always ask executives when meeting them for the first time is, what is the vision for your team this year and in three years' time? What does success look like? This is critical when hiring within teams, especially in ensuring that new starters share the same values. This drives alignment and focus. For every "Group" to become a "Team," they need something to focus on together, and to understand why their part in that team is so important to achieve the bigger picture. This is fundamental in creating a winning mentality and a successful culture. It also gives the group a purpose, focus and something to go back to during the highs and lows. The values that you create should directly underpin your vision and the company's mission. It is critical that everyone understands those values and adheres to them, otherwise they will not work successfully in the team or with others.

Remember that for every goal, there is a finishing line. It can clearly be measured. Your team often knows where, how and when they get there. A true vision is a long term big picture that should inspire people to understand the journey, and may not have a finishing line. True visionary leaders such as Jeff Bezos, Mark Zuckerberg, Jacinda Ardern, Steve Jobs or Sir Alex Ferguson, create visions that underpin behaviour and stand the test of time.

Good examples include Steve Jobs' mission statement at Apple, which was "To Change the World," and Mark Zuckerberg's Facebook mission statement; "To give people the power to build a community to bring the world closer together." These provide inspiration and often, you cannot really measure the success, but you can feel it.

Think to yourself;

Vision - Why are we here and what do we want our future state to be?

Mission - What actions need to happen?

Values - How we operate.

Now, it is important to add that if you are part of a wider group or company, the vision and values must always compliment and align with the enterprise ones. It could be leading a sales team within a company or managing one restaurant in a chain. But it doesn't mean that you cannot have a clear vision of what you expect from your people and team.

2.1 Vision

The best way to create a clear vision is to think of where the team or business should be, and work back from that. Or think, "What does success look like?" This is what our future state should look like and it is important to understand how it will make you feel. Visions tend to work for a period of time and will need re-visiting down the road, especially if they are achieved or if factors change. A vision can be a short, simple statement or be complicated and detailed - as long as people can get behind it, it can work. It needs to be specific, so you clearly identify when you have got there. It's best to follow the steps below:

Step 1: What is the Current State? - Where you are now? It could be a very grim or great place, but what are the facts? Look at the current team, revenue and market conditions. Start to understand where you are and how to attack this.

Step 2: Gap Analysis - How far away is the goal and what do you need to do to reach it? This is often a time to look at which resources are required, who are your competitors and what changes you need to make quickly. The great question at this stage is, what could stop you from being successful? You then need to overcome these factors through obstacle analysis.

Step 3: Clear Vision - What is the future state, why we are here and what we are trying to achieve? What does success look like? It needs to be communicated effectively so your team can buy into it.

Step 4: The Actions - This means addressing and creating the tasks that need to be undertaken. Tackle any self-limiting beliefs within the group.

Step 5: Success or Failure - The review of outcomes and re-evaluation of the next step. Being persistent and a change of approach is required to get back to the desired vision.

Your created vision should always be;

Measurable – Can you actually review it by numbers? For example, from customer feedback, sales numbers or downloads? It is important to be able to actually see how close or far away you are from the vision you set. Many successful visions can be purely based on financial statements, which works for a period of time and as long as they have the detail behind them. Another good example are goals related to customers directly, where you can use customer data to measure success. When you think back to Climbing Everest as a vision, getting to base camp or higher is measurable. Is 100 units your sales base camp?

Realistic – People will only buy into something they can believe in, or more importantly, you can convince them of. It's very important to look at where the business is now and create something that they can see happening at some point down the road. Being honest and realistic is always better than creating something totally unattainable. It is important to think back to the "Me" leader in their bubble. They may believe in a vision, but no one else does; they are just not telling them.

Stirs Positive Emotions – It may sound strange to say, but if you can actually connect people to what you are trying to achieve emotionally, it makes a huge difference. A clear statement and vision can achieve this. A huge proportion of large corporate companies including Apple, Cisco, Facebook, Google and Lenovo set missions that their employees engage with emotionally. It makes them feel good, and have a sense of pride and belonging to achieve this. I would say that often these are more than just number related, and need to connect with people's internal motivation.

Timeline - Every vision needs a start and end date. It is important that there is a review point when necessary, to see how close or far away you are from the goal. Team vision should run in three or four year cycles ideally, as it will take around two years to make any real form of impact in a business. Most highly successful teams achieve greatness in their third or fourth year. People need to believe you're going to hang around long enough to actually achieve the vision and get the result.

Reward – To be direct, the "what's in it for me" culture is huge right now, especially with Millennials or Gen Y staff. Make sure you are ready to feed into it with your style and vision. Your vision must have a reward for the people that are getting you there. The reward does not need to be huge; team success does not always end with a trophy and victory parade. It could be an extra days' holiday, beers on a Friday or getting lunch in for the team. Celebrate wins on the way to Everest!

Feels Natural - It is critical that your vision becomes your obsession and it comes naturally to you; you have to want it. It can start as a whisper or be hiding in the background, steadily becoming louder. It's something you feel, you're calling or something you're aspiring for that will give you gratitude/happiness.

2.2 Values

Good leaders with good values attract good people. So what are the values? They are the core staff principles that everyone must follow, and must rule the line between acceptable and unacceptable within your team. Values are also often ingrained within a person and can be very difficult to change. Some people will always be late, some people will always be victims, and some people will always be negative or selfish. Understand that most people's character has already been established when they arrive at your door. Great leadership is working with the key values and characteristics of a person, and improving them. This is often leveraging someone's greatest strength and silencing their weaknesses, so it is important to decide on values that match you as a leader. Values also drive culture. The best group of individuals I have ever managed, performed well because all of our values were aligned. People did not have the same interests, religion or beliefs, but all had the same values and it immediately worked. They should underpin hiring, firing, promotion, tasks, communication and all key decisions you make. It is important that people understand the values you have decided, and if broken, it is discussed.

Some good examples of values include;

Positive Attitude

Flexibility

Reliability

Organisation

Results Focused

Solution Focused

Punctuality

Decision Making

Personal Ownership

Excellence

Good Communication

Professionalism

Willingness to Learn

Teamwork

How does it feel for Values Not to be Honoured?

A key thing to understand is what happens if values are broken by an individual, or not honoured by the team. Often, if this is allowed to happen, people disengage rapidly and the issue will need to be addressed quickly. Some of the core values I always had in my teams were open communication, positive attitude and reliability. Running any team, people need to turn up otherwise nothing can move forward. Unfortunately, in many SMEs reliability is a huge issue with staff, especially people who are maybe in their first or second job. Negative culture spreads like cancer, and as soon as one or two people start to play up, you're lowering the bar and accepting a new lower level of behaviour. Every action has a ripple effect, and people always notice. You need to hold to your values and demonstrate your commitment to them in your actions.

2.3 Build Pride in the Group

If all of the above has happened, you should start to build your teams' identity and a sense of pride within the group. But this only happens when a team understands the vision, works to the same values and knows that their contribution matters. Team identity builds rigor against setbacks, and will increase the sense of belonging for all of the members. Team members are proud to be part of the group and often, totally engaged with the goals. It is important to understand what increases and decrease pride in the group.

Improving Team Identity

Team Name	It is critical that the name can be something to be proud of. It may be that you work for a huge business like Apple, but this does not mean that you cannot have a unique name or nickname. You want people to know what it means to be part of that team.
Team Events	You have to plan and run events outside of work. This could be attending events or planning them; ensuring that everyone attends and enjoys them. This brings a sense of purpose and fun into the group.
Standards	Make sure that there is a standard that everyone is focused on. Everyone understands where the standard sits, and new team members must work to it. It could be that you are recruiting from a different

	team, which was previously unsuccessful. When that person joins your team, make sure that they understand there is a standard.
Early Wins	Successes and wins always improve identity. So it is important to look at the milestones you are hoping to achieve, and hit them. If people feel that others are successful and they are part of a successful team, trust me, they feel a strong sense of identity.
Team Rituals	Never underestimate the importance of rituals within your team. There are hundreds of examples in sport, where rituals galvanize teams to the next level. Find where you can build rituals and make them part of a positive identity.
Shared Clothing & Products	This does not mean having a uniform in the office. It is, however, well known that shared products and clothing make people have a sense of belonging and increased loyalty.

Celebrate Everything (that is worth celebrating)	Anything good is worth celebrating inside and outside of the office. This could be a team member's first deal, career milestone, wedding or new child. It is important to make sure that your team celebrates the event, as this helps improve team solidarity.

What can Break Team Identity?

The Bad Egg	All teams occasionally have a negative or bad performer sneak through the processes and enter the team. The "bad egg" has a huge impact on identity. They often lower standards and trample on the values of the group. This needs to be carefully monitored, and the person removed quickly.
Failure	It is clear that continuous failure, however high team morale is at the beginning, wears teams out. Often failure will happen. Teams need to be resilient enough to get through the first few stages of failure because they understand the

	longer term plan. You cannot allow failure to affect the long term vision.
Bullying & Negative Banter	Every team needs a sense of humour and some banter occasionally. But there is a huge difference between banter and focused bullying or harassment. Unfortunately, often the fate created for people becomes their reality. So if someone is the butt of every joke, it means they may struggle to become successful. I have seen banter kill potential much more often than I have seen it create a winning environment.
Lack of Trust	Trust is obviously extremely important within a team, but sometimes it breaks down as a consequence of a large event or many small ones. You need to make sure that everyone trusts each other to deliver their end of the bargain.

Poor Communication	Communication is the key to keeping a team aligned. When people are left in the dark or do not feel the group is open, morale will soon decrease. Make sure everyone is communicating openly to keep an identity.
No Fun	The reality of a team is that people are happier when they are having fun. You need to make sure that you have some fun in the calendar, especially during a difficult period or after a big win. Fun creates positive endorphins and those joint stories which keep the group happy.
Harbouring Grievances	There are always grievances within a team. It naturally happens when you try to achieve a difficult goal. It is very important to not allow these to harbour themselves, and that they are openly addressed.

Summary

- Make sure that you have clarity of vision and values, as this is fundamental to your teams' engagement and success.
- Ensure that the vision is communicated effectively and regularly.
- Upholding values is a critical role for an effective leader.
- Dealing with inappropriate behaviour is essential for success.
- Focus on building pride and purpose within the group.
- Understand where you are. Know and ensure the right actions are in place to move you to your vision.

Chapter 3: The We, the Me and the Victim

"Leaders think and talk about solutions. Followers think and talk about the problem." Brian Tracy

3.1 Staff Facts

Hopefully by now you have started to think about what type of leader you are or want to be and what you want your team to achieve. But what about the people in the team; their styles, motivation and engagement levels? In the next two chapters, we will be looking at motivating, coaching, improving engagement and helping your staff to realise their potential. You will have no doubt heard, or seen, the performance explanation "'A Player', 'B Player' and 'C Player'". It's very common in US technology companies worldwide to segment their staff, and I have seen this become more common here in Europe. As a leader, you will always have a mixture of people, profiles, engagement and skill base within your team. It is important to focus on weeding out the C players or moving them up the performance ladder. You also have to understand that form can be temporary, based on timing, product, motivation or the team they are in. Some people are always world class - whatever situation they are in. They always come through as a winner. Creating the environment that encourages all to reach their full potential is critical. One A player cannot win the league title, you need a balance of skill level all people pulling in the same direction.

Everyone's Selfish

To start with, I want to tell you something you do not want to hear, but may know. It's naive to think people will follow your vision without having something in it for themselves.

Everyone, (including you), is selfish and will only be part of something if they get a reward out of it, especially in business or sport. If you think about elite sports stars, their goal is often to win a championship. The drive for success is for them first, and the team/club second. Everyone's drive is for themselves first and others after - why shouldn't it be? This does not mean people are bad employees or not team players - quite the opposite. It means there has to be something worthwhile for them in the mission. What am I going to get out of my career here? If the answer is nothing, then why are they still here? Your role is to make people understand that through working as a team, greater achievement can happen than would ever happen through one person's output. I am a believer that when you create and build a team, three types of initial profiles tend to show themselves very quickly in response to your vision and management style.

Me Thinker; they are totally focused on themselves and nothing else. When you present your vision, their first thought is - how's this going to affect me? Will I get more commission or a promotion? They tend to be very driven people and want to push you and the group for their own reasons. These people are not unwanted. You need them because they are often extremely successful in individual contributor roles. In fact, in my experience, the best five people I have managed have been 'Me Thinkers' - but work with them, not against them. It is key that you get them on-board and spend extra time with them to outline your objectives and what part they can play. Take time to answer their questions, build a relationship and always be honest. If they are engaged, they will pull people with them as they want success, reward and trophies.

We Thinker; having said earlier that everyone is selfish the next group appears to contradict this. However, the 'We Thinkers' understand that success comes from working with others, and that our own goals are often only achieved by the support of others. These people are the absolute backbone of the group and business. They are strong team players, who understand why their part is important and often understand the big picture. They tend to be happy working with anyone, have good longevity in companies, are loyal and perform consistently. You need these people. They are very important; they are the glue and the fabric to the goal. It doesn't mean these people are not selfish - their careers still matter and they still want success for themselves.

The Victim; these people say it's never their fault, they're just the victim of circumstance. Complaining and blaming others is their speciality. Often, they refuse to analyse their own behaviours and beliefs to see reality, and therefore are not open to criticism and change. This makes it difficult to break the cycle. 'Victims' want company and will often try and draw others into their club. These clubs spread quickly and need to be addressed or broken up urgently. It is important to not give up on these people, and understand what's got them to this point. How can you help them break the cycle, and how can they be part of what you are trying to achieve? Sometimes, people enter this period due to an event, lack of trust or situation that plummets them into it. We will talk about managing and coaching these people in the next chapter, but they need to be dealt with to get to Everest. Take the mind-set of looking at what someone could be, not what they are like now.

3.2 Importance of Accountability

The key tool to understand the competency of your team, is accountability and the level of intervention needed to complete tasks. When managed correctly, accountability can increase your team members' performance, skills and confidence. This is the best way to make staff feel important and valued, as ownership means they are in control of their own destiny. This could range from a whole set of scenarios including basic tasks, complex enquiries or critical customer issues. Accountability is a key benchmark in how independent and successful they are, and can uncover key training areas. For example, if they have the ability to manage an entire customer journey from enquiry to close without your input - you have a strong performer. Staff that are going to perform to the highest standards will demonstrate the ability to accept accountability for their work and their own results.

Type	Team Member Character	Manager Action
Star Performer	Make it happen despite the setbacks, have a track record of success in any situation, team or context. Likeable, high energy and results driven. It takes a huge amount of effort to stay at this level.	Give the big important jobs to them. Ensure they work with less skilled or less confident members of staff to train them and give visibility into how things are done correctly. Ensure suitable recognition for their outstanding performance. Keep them challenged and excited by demanding tasks.
Excellent Performer	Embrace the challenge and work to find a solution most of the time. Have a good knowledge	Should take on important, key tasks when they need to be delivered reliably. Give them the

	base and own the task completely. Reliable, strong team player and keen to achieve results. They are positive and enthusiastic people who are great around others.	opportunity to inspire others and motivate them.
Proactive	They are proactive and look ahead to minimise issues and ensure results are delivered. Engage well with others to help support them in their activities.	Give clarity on results expected, and ensure regular communication and positive feedback.
Responsible	Trustworthy and someone who understands reality. Tends to try and get the job done.	Provide guidance and support. Give feedback to them on how they could do

	Sometimes they lack the ability to solve complex problems.	better when reviewing their outcomes. Pair with top performers to increase visibility and raise their confidence.
Frustrator	Has all the ability and knowledge to complete tasks, but tends to need pushing and can be lazy. Struggles to reach their full potential.	Find ways to motivate them and look for their intrinsic motivation factors. Give them confidence to deliver and make mistakes, as long as they are learning from them.
Reactive	Does not really want to take any accountability for their actions. They either wait or hope that the problem will go away or someone else	Make sure they understand the benefits of planning and organisation. Explain the balance between proactive and reactive tasks, and good time

	will solve it. So they do just enough to stay in the team.	management.
Victim	Always has an excuse for poor results and nothing is ever their fault. It does not take much effort to be at this level.	Explain clearly the role and responsibilities along with the deliverables. Demonstrate to them that they are responsible for their workload, and others are doing it so why can't they? They need to accept accountability for their actions and results.
Totally Powerless	Blames others and does not know the answers to anything. Is just floating around powerless to circumstance. Often have	Ensure they are adequately trained for their role and understand what is expected of them. Give them easier tasks to build confidence

	separated themselves from reality and don't even know what's happened. Totally disengaged from the business and not willing to take any accountability.	to see if they can make it. May need to be replaced if not learning.

3.3 Favouritism and Top People

The "Dreaded" Favourite

It's happened, you've got a favourite...The dreaded problem when someone in your team is significantly better than the rest, so therefore is given more opportunities to shine. But how does it happen? They are open to change, hard-working, trustworthy, successful, and you have a good relationship with them. It happens in every team and as the pressure increases, you often rely upon the favourite more. They tend to get more inside information and scope than anyone else. You need to be aware that there is a very fuzzy line between favouritism and fairness. But generally, favouritism is bad for morale as it fosters conflicts, moves goal posts, creates poor trust and discourages competition for promotions. Here are nine steps to manage favouritism;

1) **Do not build the team or business around the favourite,** build it around an objective. You see this happen in professional sports teams when they build a team around a player and of course, in some context, for example Messi, Ronaldo or Michael Jordan, it can work. But let's get serious here, if you pivot your entire strategy or start to take big

action based on just one person, you will have some kind of a negative effect on others. I have seen this often when a new leader joins a business, and the shareholders fall in love with all they have to say. But, there is no guarantee that the favourite is going to hang around forever or be correct in what they are actually doing. So be very careful about making drastic changes too quickly, and consider the wider picture.

2) **Ask for everyone's input.** It is very easy with a favourite to just focus on them and what they think, as you may value their opinion more. But if you are making a group decision where all are affected, it's good to ask for everyone's input and allow all to feel valued.

3) **Provide development opportunities and criteria.** Make sure that everyone has the same opportunity to grow in the company. It's important to build career and competency frameworks so that everyone can apply or achieve the same criteria to get promoted.

4) **What happens in the pub, stays in the pub.** We all naturally make friends at work, but this must not affect real work decisions. Those who socialize together should not get

ahead over those who do not. This needs to be managed correctly so that everyone is equal in the workplace and there is transparency.

5) **Find systems to manage workflows**. Main examples when favouritism tends to rear its head, is during a task, work, project, or account distribution. It's important to manage this, as you trust and value the favourite. Therefore, they will be more likely to get the high profile tasks. You cannot put your business or role at risk by not giving it to them, as often, they will be the best person to do the job. You need to find a way to manage work distribution. Make sure that everyone gets their chance on better tasks or projects where you can mentor or coach them effectively. You can of course, also pair the favourite with someone to work the task together. This keeps both parties happy so they can have a shared win.

6) **Don't shine the light on them (all the time).** It's very easy to shine a light on the favourite, which means sometimes talking about their success and results. However, make sure that whilst doing this, you talk about everyone who contributed and give shared praise to each member of the team.

7) **Hold them to the Same Rules.** Make sure the same values and rules are followed by everyone. It's likely that the favourite does follow them as they are successful, but make sure they are held to the same standards as everyone else.

8) **Instil time equality.** Your time should be appropriately spread across the team and individuals based on their skill and needs. It's important to not only focus on the top or worst performers. Make sure everyone gets a fair share of time.

9) **Communicate clearly.** Explain clearly why you have made the decision to promote a member of staff. Explain why this is appropriate and what they have done to justify your choice. The more information you can give around promotions and staff changes, the better.

So What Makes a Top Performer?

Whatever you want to call them, A-Players, Star Performers or World Class - rock star people are great and need to be kept. It is important to understand what makes them so good for two reasons. One, so you can retain them within the business and keep them interested and excited about their future. Two, you can use these people to improve others and the overall success of the business. One top performer is worth three or four average performers. Top people pull others in the right direction, and can have a big positive unseen impact on the group. There are eight key traits that tend to separate these people.

- **Accept Responsibility;** successful people accept responsibility for their lives and the results in them. They accept 100% responsibility for themselves and their actions. They understand they are in control of how they respond to life and events that happen to them.
- **Future Orientation;** these people think about where they are going, are focused on the future, and create a clear vision. They build an exciting picture for themselves and take steps to make it happen. They focus on what can be done today to bring the future goal closer.
- **Goal Focused and Organised;** planning every day in advance, these individuals are clear about their priorities and important tasks that need to be done each day. They have clear written goals, often daily, weekly, quarterly and annually. They stay focused, and work on them every day. They

understand the importance of time management and how to balance their time to deliver the result expected of them.

- **Excellence Orientation;** peak performers aim to be excellent in their current job, amongst the top 10% in their chosen field. They aim to become a high performer and key player in the company. They want to have the pressure and ownership of key tasks. This will allow them to openly address and work on their weaknesses. They understand how to play to their strengths. These individuals like to live outside their comfort zone to grow and develop.

- **Solution Mind-Set;** recognising that life is full of problems which may never disappear is a key trait of these people. They do not get bogged down with unnecessary issues, and problems are dealt with in a calm and focused way. Peak performers think about solutions most of the time. These people ask, 'What happened?', 'What do we do?', 'What is my next action?' and 'How can I reduce the consequences?' They focus on what can be done, not who is to blame. They know they can handle any problem they may face. They take responsibility for how they respond to the situation.

- **Results Driven;** high performers are super results orientated. They value achievement and understand the activity that needs to happen to deliver the outcome required. Able to prioritise high value activities, they can understand what the best use of their time is.
- **Action Focused;** taking positive and constructive action, they have a sense of urgency, a bias for focused action, and make things happen.
- **Personal Growth;** keen to develop themselves and looking for opportunities to enhance professional growth, these individuals wish to learn the skills to enable them to achieve their goals

Remember this summary. A player's create tomorrows news. B players have today's news. C players talk and read about yesterday's news like it is todays.

3. 4 No Two People are the Same

As we have discussed so far, leadership is always down to context and you need to regularly flex based on situations that occur. This is the same for the people who work for you - you can have values and performance metrics that underpin the team, but everyone is different. How you manage one person will not be the same as another; good relationships are unique. It is important to recognize how your staff think and to understand their personality traits. Only through this action, can you try and get the most out of them. Remember, people are unique individuals and are not robots. I have found that lots of different personality types often work better together. Too much of the same can often cause more issues and conflict.

To lead an individual to their maximum potential, you need to truly take the time to understand them. Factors include their personality type, personal situation and their motivation to perform.

What is their Personality Type?

There are different ways of analysing personality types. A couple to be aware of are: Myers-Briggs Type Indicator and the Four Colour Personality Framework.

Staff will inevitably have different personality types depending on many factors, including nature and nurture. It is very useful to have an appreciation for the different personality types you may have to deal with. The way you interact, manage and motivate them will be dependent on their personality. One of the most frequently used personality types is based on the Myers-Briggs Type Indicator, which has been in common use for some time. This assessment will indicate which one of sixteen personality types the person belongs to. It is well accepted and tested in a business environment as a highly valued tool.

In the Myers-Briggs Type Indicator, people undertake a test and are asked a series of questions. From the individual's response, the personality type which best describes them is indicated.

The personality type is indicated by four letters representing preferences in four different categories.

Each category has two options at opposite ends, these are:

1. **Extraversion (E)** or **Introversion (I)** - Which is based upon where they focus their attention.

Extraversion – People who are Extroverts tend to focus their attention on the outer world of people and things.

Introversion – People who are Introverts tend to focus their attention on the inner world of ideas and impressions.

2. **Sensing (S)** or Intuition **(N)** – Which is based upon the way people take in information.

Sensing – People who prefer Sensing tend to take information through the five senses and focus on the here and now.

Intuition – People who prefer Intuition tend to take in information from patterns and the big picture and focus on future possibilities.

3. **Thinking (T)** or **Feeling (F)** – Which is based upon the way people make decisions.

Thinking – People who prefer Thinking tend to make decisions based primarily on logic and on objective analysis of cause and effect.

Feeling – People who prefer Feeling tend to make decisions based primarily on values and on subjective evaluations of person-centred concerns.

4. **Judging (J)** or **Perceiving (P)** – Which is based upon how people deal with the outer world.

Judging – People who prefer Judging tend to like a planned and organised approach to life and prefer to have things settled.

Perceiving – People who prefer Perceiving tend to like a flexible and spontaneous approach to life and prefer to keep their options open.

From the personality type test answers, the 4 letters that describe the person taking the test are produced. For example, ESTJ is an Extrovert, Sensor, Thinker and Judger. This Personality Type describes the person quite well and can be very useful in understanding the way they think and see the world. It is well worthwhile if practical, to get a personality type test done to help you understand your staff better and build a more collaborative relationship.

Another approach built around the model of personality was identified by Carl Jung is; the Four

Colour Personality Framework. This is useful and compliments the Myers-Briggs Type Indicator. It segments personality type into one of four colours, which can give you a broad understanding of your staff.

Type of Person	Characteristics	How they Complete a Task
Red People	Tend to be dynamic, competitive, determined, dominant, and action orientated. They often have low attention to detail but drive to get the job done. They can be controlling and intolerant.	The red people will be driven and will want to get the job done, but you may need to check the thoroughness of their work.

Blue People	Are more analytical, cautious, precise, deliberate, and deal with the facts. They have good attention to detail and strong organisation skills. They can be cold and reserved.	The blue people will be well organised but may be too detail orientated, so make sure the level of work is appropriate to the task.
Green People	These are friendly, caring, patient, encouraging and concerned about people as a priority in their thinking and decisions. They can be plodding and docile.	The green people will tend to get distracted by others, and need to be focused on their own deliverables.
Yellow People	Generally are creative, innovative, sociable,	The yellow people can go off task by seeking

	enthusiastic and persuasive. They are good at finding solutions and having new ideas. They can be excitable, flamboyant and frantic.	extra or different ways of working. This may be good but could potentially not get the job done. Keep them motivated but on task through regular check-ins.

What is their Personal Situation or Home Life Like?

It's very important to understand someone's home life and personal situation as best you can. Obviously, this is not about being intrusive, but a good open leader should encourage people to feel able share with them. Understanding your team members' circumstances at home can help you navigate and improve your relationship with them. If someone, for example, needs to finish early to pick up the children or is a sole provider, it helps in understanding their motivation and task mind-set.

3.5 Motivation

Creating high motivation for an individual or a team is an absolute must skill to be a good leader. You have to motivate through enthusiasm and finding the 'why' in people. Your staff's level of motivation will directly correlate to the level of engagement, effort and fundamentally, success you have. If a team is highly motivated, they are significantly more likely to succeed. It's not a guarantee, but high motivation and output often leads to good luck. The keys to driving motivation is to stick to some basic principles but never punish failure, as a lot of motivation is connected to confidence. If there is a confident belief something can happen, the motivation will no doubt be high.

How to Increase Motivation

Clear Direction	Have an absolute clear goal and direction that they should be aiming for. This should connect to the 'why' and the 'what' behind the objective.
Accountability	During the leadership flex, we talk a lot about accountability. But unless people have total responsibility for something, they will have limited

	motivation. The idea that no one is going to save them and they are the driving force, is a very strong motivator.
Expectations	It's really important that there is an expectation on the person to achieve said goal. Having expectations will increase motivation significantly. These expectations can come from the team, or you.
Enthusiasm	You as a leader, have to be enthusiastic. If you cannot get revved up, your team will not be able to get excited about achieving whatever goal is in front of them.
Rewards & Achievement	Having or creating a reward and sense of achievement is critical to increasing motivation. Any team must feel that if they achieve something, they will get something back.

Types of Motivation, what Drives/Motivates Someone?

It's key to understand what someone's actual motivation is, and this can be split into intrinsic, extrinsic, short and long term. Often, people will have a preference for one, but of course, based on personal circumstance this can change during different stages of their career. It's important to sit down with each member of your team and understand what their drivers are, so you can manage them effectively.

Intrinsic: factors include internal motor, achievement, social status, sense of competence, sense of progress, pride, desire to learn, fulfilment, power, fun and happiness.	Extrinsic: factors include pleasure from being seen, fame, rewards such as money and commission. Fear of punishment, consequences and being disciplined.
The Marathon Runner: long term goal and reward focused.	The Sprinter Mind-set: people who are driven by short term incentives.

People who tend to have mapped out every step to the big picture and achieve them slowly but surely. Produce good quality work and have strong intrinsic motivation - they want to do a good job for themselves, and gain a sense of achievement.	Tend to live quarter to quarter or even month to month to stay motivated, often with no real big picture but intense short-term pictures. Need a lot of praise, rewards for good actions and love incentives to achieve tasks. Focused more on extrinsic factors such as money, commission and praise from the team. For example, setting an early finish on a Friday for achievement of a task, would motivate this person.

Power of Inspiration

The feeling of inspiration is much more powerful than just motivation. Inspiration lifts you up, whilst motivation moves you forward. Inspiration is the ability to increase engagement and enthusiasm through dedication to an idea. But most importantly, your own total commitment to an objective that transfers through the team. Often, inspirational leadership builds a winning mentality and a group that totally believe they can achieve their goals, no matter what happens. Inspirational leadership means that you make someone want to do something for strong intrinsic reasons, and often with a huge sense of pride. It creates the mental process to feel you can achieve something. Finally, inspiration is the long term, big picture.

3.6 Hiring

As a leader you will need to build teams through hiring, firing and retaining talent. Hiring great people is a key responsibility and can be one of the most exciting parts of your job. New talent brings energy, ideas and impetus through the door. It gives you a chance to learn from the last person you hired and do a better job the next time. The reality is, the more your team grows, the more you learn. Always remember, one great person can make a huge shift in the positive dynamic of the group, but a bad hire can do the same in a negative way.

As an ambitious leader, hiring good people will often be the measure of you. Every great leader needs to be surrounded by like-minded people. I have worked with, and met many managers who actually dislike hiring, and that is usually down to slow or negative experiences when building their team. It is so important to be positive, and remember a leader's success is often judged by the team they build. Let's focus on some tips when hiring.

Move Quickly and Sell to Good People

First things first, let's talk about good people. You will probably meet one or two a year. It sounds low, but it is my honest opinion and lots of experienced executives would agree. How often do really good professionals become available? These are the people who are serial winners. You have to remember that they will have many options because they are always in high demand. You need to move the process quickly and show that you are interested in them. It is also important to focus on selling to these candidates. Take the time to explain where they would fit in the overall mission, and how important their part could be. When you hire one, enjoy it! They are the best people to work with and so much fun to lead.

Some Quick Metrics to Follow

There are only two real metrics to keep an eye on when hiring; time and quality. Firstly, how long has the headcount actually been open? Here, we are looking at the average time it takes to fill an open role. The key is to try and close open headcount within 6 to 8 weeks. This is just over a month and if considered, it could be a quota carrying or critical replacement, leaving the backfill open for 2 to 3 months. Naturally, if the backfill was in mainland Europe the period would be considerably longer, but that is generally down to notice periods being 3 months. I have worked with many companies who have had open headcount for up to 6-12 months. It cripples growth and burns hours of time.

Secondly, interview to hiring ratios. Wasting hours of your life interviewing the wrong people is painful. You are busy and need to focus on your critical tasks to take your team forward. That said, the reality is that you will need to interview a few candidates to understand more accurately what you are looking for. A fair ratio should be six candidates per role you have open. This may seem a lot, but is a fair metric in today's changing climate. Any more than this something is going wrong in the sourcing stage from your internal team or recruiters. It also could be that you need to slightly change the competency or responsibilities of the role you are looking for.

Focus on Backfills First

You generally have two types of roles you will hire for. These are backfills/replacement and expansion/growth positions. I would say that with all of the companies and leaders I partnered with, focusing on backfills is way more important. The reason for this is that replacement hires are already budgeted for and you are very unlikely to get quota relief if your financial year has started or has already been signed off. This means that you could be carrying the target or efficiencies for someone that does not actually exist, for as long as the role is not filled. The direct effect of this, of course, is that you are more unlikely to miss targets and other members of the team will need to overcompensate for the open recruitment. Focus on backfills quickly.

Hire on Culture and Hunger

Without any doubt in my mind, you need to build teams and hire new staff based on their cultural fit. So, what is "someone's hunger?" I believe this comes down to a person's desire, motor, work rate and drive to be successful. You often see that this is aligned to the timing within their life. Some people are great forever, and have a big appetite to stay at the absolute top of their game. Whilst for others, this only comes for a certain period of time and they can be burned out or have already achieved everything they wanted. It is very important that you understand someone's drive to succeed today, and in the next few years. Just because someone employed by your direct competitor had the drive five years ago, it does not mean they will necessarily have the same drive tomorrow working for you. Assessing their hunger is absolutely critical.

As a leader, you should be able to tell very quickly if someone fits into the culture of your team or the team you are looking to build. To assess this, always try and understand someone's value systems. If they share many of the same values as the business they are in, they are likely to succeed.

Focus on Alignment in Interviews

During an actual interview process, it is important to have total alignment between the management team and the panel who speak to the candidate. As a professional applying for a position, there is nothing worse than conflicting feedback or views from different members of the business. It is one of the biggest put-offs. Make sure that the interview processes are clear and everyone understands what the business is looking for. I would also advise four to five stages within the processes, and making the interviews of value. It is much better to have five interviews at an hour each, and really understand each candidate. This is much better than nine or ten shorter interviews that are high level engagements, but with little value.

Be Careful of the Panel Stage Roulette

It is becoming more and more common for companies to now have "panel stages" or "presentation stages" within interview processes. This is generally to assess how someone prepares, researches and executes a task. It of course gives you an insight into how they conduct themselves in a formal meeting environment too. It is very important that if you are going to introduce this stage, it actually has direct relevance to the role the person would be performing every day. Too often, I have seen companies get blown away by a good presentation from a bad candidate. This stage of the process can start to become a game of roulette. Who survives, wins. You need to use the panel to assess people's desire to execute on the set-out plan. Think how many 30/60/90 plans were never seen again after that great presentation. Always be careful of panel roulette.

If You're Not Excited, Don't Bother

Building your team is so much about trusting your gut and feelings. I personally hired my teams with one principle. If you're not excited don't bother. You should be waiting at the door for your new member of staff to join, ready to build their career and get them embedded in the business. There should be a sense of excitement and anticipation. If you do not feel this, then do not bother hiring them. It is not fair on you or them, and will only result in a total waste of everyone's time.

Always be Interviewing

One of the most important lessons you learn as a leader is that things are always changing, and the faster you can react to that, the better. You should always be interviewing and networking with relevant professionals. A good rule is to interview one person a week, even when you are not hiring. This could be a casual coffee or phone call with a relevant professional. This is only four hours a month, and the reality is that you will be hiring soon due to poor performance or growth within the team anyway. Always be interviewing.

Understand Someone's Journey to Date, it will Often Determine their Future

When interviewing potential candidates, always focus on their journey and their life as a total measurement. Find out about their upbringing, family, values and what goals they set themselves that have been achieved. The past is the single biggest variable to determine the future. If people have had clear goals and objectives which they have consistently achieved throughout their lives, they will do it again. So, look for patterns within people that show you who they are. Actions or proof of massive actions far out-weigh the words spoken.

Take References

Taking reference is so incredibly important when hiring someone, for a number of reasons. I have met so many leaders who did not take them or have left it for someone else to do so. This is incredibly lazy on many levels. Taking references will help you to understand someone's character and performance to date; the good, bad and great within their skills set. It will help you identity issues quicker. Often, candidates will provide two or three references. Always make sure one is from a former boss with credibility. I also often see people pass friends or irrelevant colleagues as references. This is unlikely to truly help you determine the person's ability to do the role, or how you can help them improve. Always take references.

Watch out for the "Fussy Closer"

When closing someone to join you, it is very important that the candidates get all the details. This includes the package, role and responsibilities. You want professionals who qualify correctly and feel totally prepared to make the change. So, what is the "fussy closer?" These are candidates who want to check every single tiny detail, and take a long time to do everything. They often ask the same question many times- things that have been covered previously in the process at least once before. They tend to focus on details that are often not really relevant for the position they are taking. They also do not see the opportunity in front of them, rather, "what's in it for me?" Then, they either do not join or are totally underwhelming when they eventually do. Be careful of the fussy closer, you can sense them.

Get it Right

Get it right as best you can. Hiring the wrong people wastes time, energy, resources and can have a direct effect on your customer relations. Getting it right the first time is not easy, but really worth it - focus on that.

Firing 3.7

As a leader or manager, there is nothing worse than firing people. You have to remember every working relationship starts with a positive goal, so when it ends badly, it is distressing for both parties. As we have seen during Covid-19, firing can be absolutely no one's fault but because of uncontrolled change. It can also be absolutely and totally necessary if a member of staff is not performing and is not responding to management, or conducts themselves in an unprofessional manner. Here are the rules of firing.

Always Meet Face to Face

It is a stressful time for both parties, so always meet people face to face so you can have a clean break, and can both get closure. Team members who have dedicated time to work for you, deserve the respect of you meeting them and explaining the situation.

Ensure there are Warning Signs

When firing someone, the person should never feel blindsided. You should always have performance metrics or warnings in place, so the individual has time to adjust their behaviour. You often see performance improvement plans used and if they are not met, the employee can be prepared for the inevitable fact they are getting fired. This is also why it is so important that you make notes and have a record of achievements or events.

Always have a Witness

When dismissing someone you should always have a witness. Ideally from human resources or a senior leader within the business. It is important that if there are any repercussions, it is not your word against theirs. The witness can also act as a neutral supportive individual.

Don't Labour the Point, They Get It

These types of meetings should last 30 to 45 minutes, absolute maximum. Often when you start discussing the dismissal, they get it straight away, so allow yourself the time to talk them through the decision. But do not labour the point.

Don't Leave any Grey Areas - The Decision is Final

Always remember staff have the right to appeal your decision, so make sure your rationale is clear and final. You want to make sure when leaving the meeting that they know there is no coming back, nor any need to discuss the topic again. Case closed.

Company Property and Systems

It sounds very obvious, but make sure that all the company property has been recovered, such as laptops, phones or company intellectual property. You also need to close down your online systems, such as emails.

End the Meeting on a High Note

In life, the end of one chapter leads to another, and as a leader it is important to try and end the meeting on a high note. Most people will not be bitter or upset about leaving a business after having had time to reflect. This is especially the case if you have been a good manager whilst this person worked for you, and you tried your best. You always want to stay in contact with people and remain professional. Allow for you both to take this as a chance to learn. End on a high note.

Summary

- Identity the different personality & ability types you have in the group.
- Encourage team and personal accountability for the delivery of goals.
- Ensure that you understand where your team fit in the performance ranking, and how you can move them up to the next level.
- Manage favouritism proactivity.
- Understand what makes a top performer for you and your team.
- Identify any gaps in performance and take action to address them.
- Create high levels of motivation and enthusiasm in your team.
- Focus on inspirational leadership whenever possible.

Chapter 4: Leadership Formula

"Coming together is the beginning; keeping together is progress; working together is success."
Henry Ford

So far, a large proportion of the material we have covered has been around setting your team up for success, understanding them as individuals and setting a clear vision. In this next chapter we will talk about some of the key ingredients and situations that occur. To become a master of the "leadership flex," you must understand how best to lead your team through different climates and create resilience. This should all begin with trust.

4.1 Trust

This is the absolute foundation of building relationships with your team and people. Trust is the number one tool to create success; it empowers your team and improves overall employee engagement and happiness. Trust also protects your vision and has the power to make or break the group through big moments. Remember, you are directly impacting your team's success and livelihoods, so they have to trust you. Most importantly, when you remember the difference between leaders and managers, trust is one of the key aspects. Leaders influence others and demand forward thinking that could be a long way down the road. The team must trust and believe that they can get there.

There is a common misconception that trust should be expected by a leader and their team, but I firmly believe trust is earned, not given. This works in two ways; as a leader, you have to earn the trust of your team through your actions and character. The team or person has to earn your trust through results and behaviours.

How to Build Trust

I believe that there are four simple steps to build trust-

- **Integrity;** this is absolutely critical if people are to build trusting relationships with you. You must have a strong moral and ethical purpose. Actions include keeping secrets that a team member shares with you and not letting emotions such as anger or disappointment get the better of you. You must demonstrate consistency and be accountable for the principles of the team. This ensures that you remain professional and focused at all times.

- **Communication & Transparency;** express yourself openly and give others permission to do the same. Share your thoughts honestly and often. When communicating, show clear compassion with others.
- **Be Reliable;** as a leader, it's so important to be there for your team. They have to believe you will be there when the doors open and close. Deliver on what you say you are going to do, and follow up on objectives consistently. If things need to be changed or be cancelled, call and explain why. Be on time, be organised and set the standard within the team.
- **Competence & Knowledge;** it's important that you understand what your team is actually doing so that you can intervene where possible. A key producer of trust is being able to support your team and find solutions with them. Having strong knowledge of your sector is key. If they feel that you do not know how to solve a problem, they may not bring it to your attention and therefore won't trust you so much.

Eureka Moment

I am an absolute believer in the "Eureka Moment" and you have to look for it. The "Eureka Moment" is when either your team or an individual finds trust. Trust always takes time and is created. It will often be a shared victory or shared solution to a problem that is encountered. It creates relationships and shared experiences. Teams become connected through shared experiences; as a leader, you must use these to create trust and create the "eureka moment".

4.2 Personal Communication and Engagement

Personal excellence in communication is a critical skill if you are to achieve your full potential as a leader or manager. It has been shown in numerous studies that success is more to do with our emotional intelligence than our academic intelligence. Our communication with others is through the words we use, our tone of voice but most importantly our body language.

Body language is the most powerful aspect of our communication and needs to be in alignment with the words we use and our tone. Staff can quickly see if you are not consistent between your words, tone and body language. Have an upright and open body posture, and lean forward a little into conversations to show that you are being attentive. When presenting, stand up, look up and use your hands to emphasise your points. Staff will watch your body language and infer concerns from how you appear to them. They will read things into your posture and facial expressions. You need to appear positive, calm and in control at all times, even if you are not feeling it.

Building good rapport with staff is key to great performance and an honest, open relationship. In building rapport with other people, always talk at a similar pace, tone and volume as them. This will help put them at their ease and they are more likely to be open and listen more attentively. Your body language should be positive, but as far as is practical, take the same body posture as the person you are talking with. Always seek to understand things from the other person's point of view first. Put yourself in their shoes to gain a better perspective. They are far more likely to listen to you and take on-board your message if you have demonstrated your interest in them and their situation.

4.3 Importance of Delegation

One thing you soon learn in management and leadership is the absolute importance of delegation. Understand what to do yourself, what to do with someone, and what to delegate to drive a cohesion within the team and business. It can be difficult to delegate, but remember that you have to drive accountability, and good people want ownership. It's very easy as a leader to keep control of everything because you believe you do the best job, but this is not productive. Delegation allows you to make the best use of your time and skills, and done correctly, it helps other people in the team develop. Delegation should be a win-win situation when done well. However, that does not mean that you can delegate everything. Your role needs to be split into either supportive behaviours or directive behaviours. When delegating to staff, communicate what's expected, the required results and when you expect it by. Then, check the understanding of the staff and their commitment to actually complete the task. Supportive behaviour means that you help the individual, but they are acting and conducting the task themselves. You are there to answer any questions but they are accountable for the result. Directive behaviour means that you are involved with the task, directing the activity to achieve the outcome. Your input will depend on many factors, including the skill and confidence of the subordinates, timescales, and the importance of the task. For simplicity, look at risk, value, and complexity when delegating.

The four types of delegation include;

Supportive: The task owner or group that have been delegated to make the key decisions and are accountable for the result. You can have input when required, but they make the choices and you are there to mediate. These are often low risk tasks but can be high value and complex.

Coaching: You are directly involved with the task, working on it with the team or individual. Focused on selling your ideas, but understanding that everyone's input is valid. Responsibility is generally shared; this is a chance to develop your team and their skills. They are often tasks that are of higher importance and high complexity.

Delegate: These are usually low risk, low value and low complexity tasks. You can delegate this completely so that you need minimal input. The task owner leads totally and should complete without much interference. You should be hands off and agree how much checking is required.

Direct: This is a task where you lead and are very hands on. You make the key decisions and are autocratic with actions needed. Often high value and complex. Sometimes the capabilities of staff are low, and they need clear direction and decision making for the task to be delivered. In this circumstance, they do minor activities as requested by the leader.

4.4 Managing Change

Change happens... We may not like it and it may not be our choice, but leading your team through change is a core skill in leadership. Change tends to happen because of either a choice from leadership or an unforeseen event that forces change on the business. Both these incidences cause very different reactions from you and your team. Sometimes change can be planned a long time in advance, giving you time to run scenarios and situations that may occur. But as we have seen from 2020 and Covid-19, some events are external and totally unforeseen events which you as a leader must respond to quickly, without any time to prepare. You have to be able to react and drive change quickly based on context and circumstance. Change creates uncertainty, and this is the killer of success, efficiency and trust. People would rather know a plan even if it involves change vs having any uncertainty. Depending on the event you will need to react and respond in different ways. This is mainly during the first two stages when you **evaluate** the issue and **plan** how to implement the change.

There are four events of change which you need to be aware of. The first two of these are external events/changes.

External Events; some change comes about due to factors that are not in your control and never could have been.

External Unforeseen Event: This is not planned for or chosen. They are events that you have to react to. Examples could include, a competitor receives extra funding, your largest customer gets acquired or a global pandemic such as Covid-19.

- **Evaluate:** You need to assess the impact of the event on your business, including the size and significance. This should include people, customers, extra costs, revenue change, and profitability. A full analysis needs to be conducted very quickly.

- **Plan:** Consider the range of options and approaches. Create a judgment based on the consequences and wider future impact.

External Planned Event: Planned event you may not have chosen or have control over, but have had time to plan for. Examples could include for UK businesses preparing for Brexit or an EU legislation change, Government Tax change, your company becoming acquired or received funding.

- **Evaluate:** Firstly, you need to look at what the impact is across the business. You have time to be proactive as this is a planned change. Speak to experts, seek help, and run industry wide research. You have time to reduce the impact of the change on the business.

- **Plan:** Consider the range of options and approaches. Create a judgment based on the consequences and wider future impact.

Internal; an event that happens inside the business and you had, or have, some control over. This of course can still be unforeseen, as well as planned. Often, more emotions and blame are attached to internal change because you can be held accountable. For this reason, the ability to sell this change and action quick-wins is very important.

Internal Unforeseen; this is an unplanned situation that you need to act upon. Examples could include a top performer handing their notice in, serious internal product or service failure or unseen change of circumstance for a key member of staff.

- **Evaluate:** Gather the facts and full information about the unforeseen event. Avoid an emotional reaction. Consider the fall out and significance of the event.

- **Plan:** Analyse the facts, information and current situation. Consider the range of options and approaches. Create a judgment based on the consequences and wider impact.

Internal Planned Event; this is a significant, planned change by management. Examples could include new product or service, new commission scheme, change in management structure and change in office location.

- **Evaluate:** A planned change has been decided upon and agreed by the leadership team. Be fully brought into the change as the leader of your team. Ensure you understand why it is happening.

- **Plan:** Develop an internal communication plan. Consider any risks or issues that may arise.

Whatever the circumstance external, internal, planned or unplanned the next steps are mostly the same.

- **Consult:** Discuss issues with key players and change agents. Get their feedback and get their buy-in for a new action plan.
- **Communicate:** Communicate the event and the agreed actions to the team or business. Prepare for concerns, questions and challenges as a result of the event.
- **Listen:** Listen to the concerns of staff and reassure them of a plan going forward. Analyse any resistance, ensure concerns are overcome.
- **Action:** Action the change within the team.
- **Monitor:** Follow up on change, make sure that the change has worked. Prepare or make further changes as needed.

4.5 Asking Good Questions

As we have just discussed in 'managing change', understanding good questions is a vital skill for a business leader. This is one of the critical skills to be competent at leading a group through change, handling conflict, and delegation. Good questions can help you gain a better understanding of what is going on. This enables you to get to the truth of where people are, keep on top of issues that may arise, and understand the potential risks to not achieving targets. The person who asks questions has control and it's very important that you actually listen to the answers. I have seen many leaders who interpret an answer to a question to favour their own agenda, and often miss the point. This then confuses the employee and team further. Make sure you understand the answer correctly, and challenge the response where appropriate.

Good questions should get to the centre of a problem or determine someone's mindset. This could be during a team meeting, solution discovery, appraisal or one to one. Lots of team members fall into two categories when asked questions. Firstly, the robot. Programmed to tell you exactly what you want to hear, but with no real depth or meaning behind their answers or true motivation. It's important to notice what people say and what they do. Actions are far more important than words. Showing commitment and motivation to a project or goal is much more important than "saying" you are committed. So continually assess, how do they act? What's their tonality? What are their results? I regularly sat down with sales reps and professionals who told me their goal was to buy their first property, for example. We worked out how much they would need to save up, what targets they would need to achieve and what sacrifices they would need to make to achieve that goal. Later, I would question how they were progressing against their targets, and they had often taken no action to actually achieve the set goal. Sometimes, they had even forgotten the discussion in the first place. Hence why good leaders all take notes. Questions should lead you to understand what your team's mindset and actions are.

Secondly, the statue. This person is often the total opposite to the previously explained type. These are often team members who have nothing to say or provide to a discussion. This is because they do not have the answers or have not really thought about the answers properly. It's very important to spend extra time with these types of people to really help them get to decisions and understand facts better. If they do not have the correct answer or have not prepared correctly, rearrange discussions until they actually have some information and value to add. Questions in this case should allow you to get the team member talking, and help you to understand their thought process. Great leaders ask great questions to uncover the true thoughts of their team. Good questions should move past the typical answers, and make people truly think about why things have happened and what they actually want out of something.

Open questions are important to explore situations and gain understanding. They require someone to think about the answer and give more of a response. The questions will often start with the words- What? Where? Who? When? How? Why?

Try to avoid closed questions, as they are yes and no answers. Closed questions tend to be used to qualify a task being completed. For example, 'is the report finished yet?'

Probing Questions should be used to dig a little deeper into issues that you face. Asking 'What else?' is a good question to have in your locker- 'What else do I need to know?' 'What else happened?' Using this question, there is no excuse not to get all the facts of a situation from your team.

When asking questions we are often trying to clarify our thinking and understanding of a situation. We can use questions such as:

'Can you give me an example?'

'Could you explain further?'

'What is the problem you are trying to solve?'

We need to challenge assumptions by asking:

'Is that always the case?'

'What are you assuming?'

'How could you verify or disprove that?'

'What would happen if...?'

For examining evidence and rational thinking, we might ask:

'Why would you say that?'

'How do you know?'

'Why?'

'What evidence is there that supports...?'

We should also consider alternative perspectives:

'Are there any alternatives?'

'What is the other side of the argument?'

'What makes your viewpoint better?'

'Who would be affected and what would they think?'

In considering the implications and consequences of a course of action, we could ask:

'What are the implications/consequences of?'

'How does that affect...?'

'What if you are wrong?'

'What does our experience tell us will happen?'

4.6 Coaching and Feedback

Coaching and feedback for your team and individuals is another area where you can hugely differentiate yourself from a lot of leaders. By excelling at this vital skill, you can build relationships and improve people's performance. Coaching should be done in structured sessions and at spontaneous moments where it is appropriate. Remember, most learning is done on the job in real time, so use these moments to teach.

Feedback should be given in a more structured environment, and if negative, should always be in private. Praise of course, can be given in public. Detailed feedback is good in appraisals, one to one's or monthly/quarterly business reviews. As a team, you should always hold reviews which include sharing data, results and feedback. It's important to be honest and transparent during these sessions.

During coaching and feedback, it's best to use the **RSPTA** formula. It will help you ensure that you have a consistent process, and staff will appreciate your feedback much more if done in a regular and timely way.

The first step in the process is to ensure that you have built **RAPPORT**. Connect with staff by setting the scene and putting the coached person at ease. Create a supportive, safe environment. Smile and use open body language. Build rapport to facilitate an open two-way conversation. You need to foster a collaborative approach to build trust.

The second stage in coaching and feedback is to get to a good understanding of the **SITUATION**. Ask open questions and clarify the facts of where the person is with their work and tasks. Listen carefully to what is said, and be sure to understand the challenges and issues they face.

Then you need to discuss their **PERFORMANCE**; how are they getting on? Have they displayed a good grasp of the issues and how they are doing? Check and ensure that you have not assumed anything and that you are both on the same page about how they are getting on. If you can, give examples of where you have seen strengths and where they do a good job to build their self-esteem. What can they learn from their experiences to help them in the future?

Having got agreement about current performance, the next step is to clarify **TARGETS** and expectations. Have they got a good understanding of their targets and their way forward to achieve them? Explain to them that you have trust in their abilities to deliver what is expected.

Finally you should help define the **ACTION** plan; put timescales next to the agreed actions. Ensure commitment from the member of staff to deliver on the actions, agree the 'how' as well as the 'what'. Reflect with them on their understanding of the feedback. What concerns do they have? Set a review date to check progress and keep going.

The Best Way Forward Formula (BWFF)

We are all faced with different issues and problems at work and in life. How we handle and deal with these is key to our success. The better our decision making process and more rigorous our thinking, the more likely we are to make progress. The 'Best Way Forward Formula' has been designed to enable you to ensure that you have made the best choice possible from your options, and have thought through clearly the action you are going to take. Leaders know that making decisions is a key skill. Although they don't always get them right, they know that at the time, based on the information available, it was the best choice. If you have made the best choice possible at the time, you can do no more.

Circumstances change events, but knowing you made the best possible choice at the time gives you confidence in the future.

To employ the 'Best Way Forward Formula,' firstly, you need to understand the situation and challenges you face. Have you clearly defined the problem and issues? Then, you need to question the situation thoroughly and ensure you have all the relevant facts available. A thorough understanding can only be achieved if the questions give you a good appreciation for the issues, challenges and problems you face.

When you have all the relevant information you can start to analyse the facts and consider options. It is important to consider the consequences and wider implications of any options or actions you might make. It is important to consider other points of view and see the issue from different perspectives. You may need to consult others or 'put yourself in their shoes' to see things from their situation.

Having done this, you can then make the best possible judgement about the situation and decide upon the course of action that is most appropriate, all things considered.

So, the 'Best Way Forward Formula' is:

1. Understand the situation.

2. Formulate your questions (What? Where? Who? When? Why? How?).

3. Gather the information/facts.

4. Analyse the information/facts.

5. Consider the consequences and wider implications.

6. Explore other points of view.

7. Form a judgment to decide on the conclusion.

8. Take the appropriate actions.

Summary

- Ensure you build trust and act with integrity in all that you do.
- Focus on being an excellent communicator to achieve full engagement.
- Understand the importance of delegation and how to use it appropriately.
- Change happens. Be prepared when you can, and when you cannot, be positive with your response and actions.
- Questions are absolutely essential to gaining a good understanding of what's actually happening, so you can make better decisions.
- Regular coaching and feedback to your team is essential if they are to achieve their full potential.

Chapter 5: Mirror Management

"We all have dreams. But in order to make dreams come into reality, it takes an awful lot of determination, dedication, self-discipline and effort."
Jesse Owens

5.1 The Skill of Managing Yourself

Hopefully, so far you have learned and started to understand how to lead your team through different situations based on context and building relationships. Great leaders understand the most important person to manage is yourself, and the effect your behaviour has on the team. You need to be conscious of leading by example, and be aware that what you do will be what's seen to be acceptable by the group. Leadership is a lot about visibility. Our behaviours will often consciously and subconsciously impact our team. Therefore, you need to focus on the good behaviour that you would want your team to adopt. It's critical that you understand yourself, and avoid the fatal impact of not managing yourself correctly. Ego and bad self-management are a key reason that teams fail. Remember that you are setting the standards and consistency that the team will follow.

There are eight elements to Mirror Management.

Emotional Self-Awareness; self-awareness plays a critical role in how we understand ourselves and how we actually relate to others. This includes understanding our own character and feelings, which is particularly important as a leader. You should be able to look at yourself objectively and understand what others think about you. Most importantly, how you affect others through your behaviours. People who are not self-aware tend to struggle with the leadership flex because they see every situation as the same even though they are often very different. This is because they do not consider the feelings of others in their decision making.

Organisation and Discipline; a key skill in leadership is to remain organised and disciplined with yourself. As a leader it is important to create good habits and routines, such as reviewing your goals and objectives, organising your day, and following up with key people. You need to make sure that you stick to your good habits and follow your agenda. Remember what it is like when your manager does not have a one to one with you for weeks, and then cancels the booked one? Bad leaders are difficult to track down; you never see them and you never hear from them. To avoid this, you need to be consistent about your reliability, respect people's time and be focused on the task.

Awareness of your own Strengths and Limits; a key skill in becoming a great leader is focusing on your strengths and understanding your limitations. It is far better to be the master at some skills, and then build a team of people who are strong in your weaker areas. This creates balance and a strong team environment. Everyone has limits and weaknesses; openly addressing them and knowing what they are is a sign of self-awareness and emotional intelligence.

Open to Feedback; good leaders have to be open to feedback of all kinds. Feedback can allow the leader to become more open and deal with some of the tension within a group. The other key aspect of feedback is that yes, it highlights improvement areas, but often it can also be a source of great confidence for you. Feedback can show that you are doing a great job and your team actually values you. There are very few thank-yous in leadership, not because people do not think of it, but often the opportunity does not present itself. Feedback on both sides, can build great relationships. Feedback is also the foundation of you looking to develop improved personal skills and enhance your own performance. Without having feedback, you cannot grow and cannot learn how to improve as a person. Fear of feedback stunts your personal growth.

Self-Confident (the power to believe in oneself); you can look in the mirror and see a kitten, but remember, you have to bring the lion to the office! There's a great phrase about faking it till you make it, and it is absolutely true. You do not need to have an answer to everything and you certainly do not need to be perfect, but you have to believe that you can achieve the goals that you are setting. It is important to understand your own self-limiting beliefs, and make sure that you address these yourself, or with a mentor.

Emotional Self-Control; control of your emotions is so important in leadership. You will often be the person to hear and deliver news first. You have to remain calm, composed and positive throughout the challenges you face. This does not mean you are a robot or have to be cold, but remain balanced and consistent. People must feel confident to approach you and discuss things with you openly, knowing you have control over your emotions. This means that you are able to make rational responses, not emotional reactions.

Restraint & Patience; it is really critical that you understand that leaders have to have appropriate restraint and patience. Whilst as the leader, you are good at the job, this does not mean that others will be able to work to your standards. You need to be patient to get the results required. Leadership should teach you the patience you need to get a result.

Learns from Experience; nothing beats experience and often, the same thing can happen multiple times within your career. You get that 'I have been here before' feeling, and think, 'what did I do last time?' Reflection is important. You need to understand what happened after an event, and what can be done differently next time if this happens again. Experiences are great teachers for you if you take the time to learn and reflect on what happened. You will become more rational and less emotional in your decision making.

5.2 Types of Decisions

One of the biggest areas of mirror management is how we make decisions, as every choice we make leads us down a different road and creates an impact. Understanding the process we use to make decisions is important, as often there are lots of factors to consider. These factors could include timing, costs, emotional reaction to an event, or they are well planned in advance with time to be thought through. There tend to be five types of decisions.

1) Instant; these types of decisions often rely on instinct, impulse and intuition. They tend to be a reaction to an event that is, or has, taken place. In general, they are not always the best decision because they can be rushed and the longer term consequences have not been considered. It is worth mentioning that often, these decisions can be made if you are in a survival mode and the event calls upon it. When managing yourself you have to understand the urgency of the event and if you need to make an instant decision.

2) Emotional; we are generally led by emotions, whether we like it or not. Quick, emotional choices can be dangerous, as feelings override rational thoughts and any previous planning goes out of the window. It is important to stop and understand when emotions have got the better of you, and reflect before acting. This is of course, not always possible, and it is key to not be void of any emotions. Sometimes using your intuition and trusting your emotions when it feels right, can lead you to a valid decision.

The key is to control negative emotions such as anger and disappointment, because they will often lead to you not making rational decisions.

3) Deferred; it is sometimes appropriate to delay a decision if waiting will enable you to get more information, or the circumstance can change for the better. This should not be a form of procrastination, but a positive choice to produce a better option later.

4) Consultative; this type of decision is good during change that is affecting people. It always involves others and is often useful to get to a stronger consensus across the group. If used effectively it can motivate the team, but can take longer and may get cynical responses. Often, once used, it can be difficult to go back as you have handed some of the power to others.

5) Rational; these are decisions that are taken considering the situation and potential implications. This is usually the best option, if you have the time to think the choice through. Often, these are thought through clearly with all the factors considered.

Summary

- Understanding and managing yourself is critical if you are to be successful.
- Organisation and discipline are key habits of great leaders.
- Focus on the lion inside you.
- Know what type of decision to make based on context, timing and controlled emotion.

Chapter 6: Accepting Failure and Disappointment

"Every adversity, every failure, every heartache carries with it the seed of an equal or greater benefit." Napoleon Hill

6.1 Difficult Roads Often Lead to Beautiful Destinations

One of the most difficult parts of being a leader is failure and disappointment. Remember, anyone who wants to do anything of any value in life will fail at some point. We sometimes wish things could have happened differently. Failure is the thing you cannot prepare for and often cannot see coming when it hits you. Unfortunately, you do lose sometimes and let's face it, life is simply not fair. You can have done everything you thought was right, and still lose. Failure acts as the single biggest teacher to improvement, and the biggest factor in building your steel and grit in leadership. If you give up after the first or second hurdle, you will never make it as a leader. People need to believe that you are going to hang around a long time and are committed enough to actually make something happen. Great leaders evaluate their success by the *impact* and added value they have within a business. This can often take years to happen. It is important to understand that you have to take accountability for failure, but understand that you need to review why you have failed. Look at all factors. There's no shortcut to success; it involves pain, failure, early mornings, late nights and the desire to keep going. If you can look up, you can get up and go again.

When evaluating failure, it's important to review several aspects to understand why.

The goal was always unrealistic; simply what you were trying to achieve was not going to happen based on you and your team's skills set.

Competitors beat you; every business has competitors and they beat you. It's important to understand why and how you can improve - make sure it does not happen again.

Organisation Environment; your style, values and energy are being driven in the wrong company. Realistically, you may always struggle to achieve your goals because you are not aligned.

You or your team did not perform well enough; sometimes when you evaluate failure, the simple truth is that you did not want it enough or perform well enough. We can often feel this and have to accept its truth.

There is nothing you could have done;
sometimes external factors such as Covid-19 or economic crisis stop you from being successful, and there is nothing you could have done. You need to review and change the plan with the new external circumstance in consideration.

Not all Great Achievements get Trophies

Most people are way too hard on themselves, especially if they are highly motivated and focused. An Olympic athlete who comes in fourth place could see that as failure, but did they do a great job just to get there in the first place? It is important to understand the task and achievement in relation to the difficulty and realistic chance of success. I always say to my team, aim for the stars and you may end up on the moon - which is still excellent. Review your achievements with their context, and in reality, you achieve them within. It is often the case that the goal was never actually achievable, so disappointment was always inevitable. I can think of some of my best achievements so far in my career that received no praise or rewards. This is because they were excellent within the context or environment that I was based in. If the best person in the world was in the same situation as you, what would they have done differently? Often very little or nothing. You have to remember that in this occupation, there may not be a trophy but there will be soon or next time. Often, what you have achieved is a step forward, towards the ultimate goal.

6.2 Organisation Environment

The world of work has changed massively. The lifetime employment of the past has long gone. Staff now need organisations that are innovative, flexible, open to change, have constant learning and continuous improvement. The organisation's culture and work environment play a massive part in your ability to be successful. The culture and behaviour of the organisation is impacted by many factors, including the history, leadership style, management systems and work methods. All organisations have developed differently, and this is seen in the way that they treat stakeholders such as customers, suppliers and employees.

The physical facilities, technology, rules and regulations, communication patterns, and political behaviour are all issues to be considered. It is clear that the business culture and environment has to be in alignment with your personal values and expectations. If you are to achieve the success you desire in the business where you work, you need to have the flexibility, power and control over your team and work.

If you are a positive, open and driven individual, keen to take action and make progress, but working in an autocratic blame culture environment, then you are unlikely to take risks and make decisions. Why would you push yourself and your team if this exposes you to criticism and blame?

Make sure that you are working in the right culture and environment. This means you have the freedom to get on with your job, without playing games and watching your back. Politics and organisational behaviours occur in every business, but make sure it is not holding you and your team back from meeting their full potential. Your personal skills and abilities can only be fully developed and utilised in the right environment. Make sure that you are in one.

6.3 The Great Leaver

Every great leader is surrounded by great people and great people are hard to say goodbye to. A great strength of a leader is that people around them improve, soak up their energy and knowledge over time. It is also really important to say that good leadership is the ability to create, and often coach people to become highly successful. This makes it even more difficult to let them leave, especially when you look at who they were when they started, to where they are now. Often, these team members will have been really good right hands through a difficult journey. Of course, this is a strength, but can feel like a curse when a great team member eventually leaves. Like it or not, really good people come in and out of your career, and it could be a few years before you work with another one again. Dealing with the loss of the "Great Leaver" can be very difficult, and can feel extremely disappointing. As discussed in the previous chapter, it is of course important to understand why the person is leaving, but sometimes there is simply nothing you could have done. When you have a great team or person, enjoy it and drive towards success because naturally, over time people need new challenges and will move on. It is not your fault and you have probably learned a lot through managing that individual. Attrition rates are something that need to be managed, and as a leader you must always be considering what could happen if key people leave.

6.4 The Comeback is More Important than the Setback

Failure does not last forever, and I can tell you that the comeback is more important than the setback. Trying and failing is the best experience to actually achieve the goal. I am sure that we can think of many examples of people, sports stars and businesses who have had a much bigger bounce back than come down. Many years ago, I had a target to build a one-million-pound market segment. During this time, I built three teams before achieving the actual goal. The final team was probably the best team of my career because I had learned from the previous mistakes.

The key is to remain hungry through failure, you have got to have grit and stick. This means stick to the task and do not lose the passion for your goals and dreams. My advice would be, remember what you came for and deliver the objective. Do not allow anything within reason to stop you.

When failure happens it important to follow these processes to help-

Accept the Emotions; the emotions that follow failure vary, but mainly focus on anger and disappointment. You need to accept that you feel how you feel. Allow yourself the time to process the emotions and do not bury them. It is important at this stage to talk to family or a mentor about what has happened. Often, this can make you feel much better about the events that took place. Do not hang around this stage too long.

Be Realistic and Examine the Truth about the Failure; be honest with yourself and examine why the failure happened. Think about the reasons listed above and your performance. It is important that you are totally open to why this has happened so that the same issue does not repeat itself later down the line.

Accept the Appropriate Level of Accountability; it is very unlikely that you are solely to blame for the failure, especially if you are part of a business or wider organisation. You need to accept the appropriate level of accountability and then start to move on.

What have I Learned; the main purpose of failure is to learn, so that when this situation happens again (or something similar), you will be ready and armed to do something different.

Take Action; you know that you need to set new goals and milestones to achieve based on what has happened. Make sure that they are realistic, and you feel confident about achieving them.

Face the Fear, Move from the Comfort Zone; move forward and face the fear. The past is the past, and has already happened. Do not cheat your future by focusing on your past.

Summary

- Failure is a direct consequence of trying to achieve something.
- Everyone has, and does, fail during their life and career.
- When failure does occur, identify the real cause.
- Learn from set-backs and build your resilience from them.
- Great people leave - do not allow this to affect your personal morale.
- Always take accountability for outcomes, whatever they may be.

Chapter 7: Choosing and Managing the Boss

"Nothing is an obstacle unless you say it is."
Wally Amos

One of the most important relationships you will
ever have in work is with your boss. It is totally true
what they say, working for a great leader is more
important than working for a great company. So
choosing a leader to work for is so important if you
want to develop your career. The truth is, some
managers see hiring new people as painful, and
when you join you are another cog stuffed into the
system, forgotten about, getting dusty. Look for a
manager who wants to invest in you, work with you,
and is a respected leader.

All relationships need to be managed. As much as
your team needs managing, so does your boss,
and upward management is very important if you
are to be successful within a business. The boss
has to trust you and see you doing a good job. It is
amazing how many people do not value this
relationship, and then wonder why opportunities
pass them by or why they do not progress as they
should. Show your leader the same respect you
would want your team to show you.

7.1 Managers to Avoid

Let's start with the type of manager you want to avoid, and the type you also do not want to be;

Mushroom Manager; fundamentally, these are people that keep everyone in the dark about what they are doing and what is going on. They tend to have a plan which only they actually know and understand. The staff do not have ideas brought forward or encouraged based on the fact that everyone is kept in the dark. It is very often a situation where one or two people are making all the choices, and not letting others know what is happening. These managers are surprised by the results of the team when they are the ones that kept them in the dark in the first place.

Seagull Manager; these people tend to hover around where the actual work is done, and instruct staff. They make lots of noise and interact with employees only when a problem arises. Generally, they tend to be quick to make decisions without really understanding what's happened, and then leave a mess behind. These managers rarely praise people, and are quick to criticise others' work before disappearing again.

Saviour Manager; these people like to be seen as the 'Chief Firefighter'. They enjoy getting stuck into problems at the last minute when they are serious enough for them to be seen as the saviour for solving them. This gives them a sense of importance and power. Often, the problems they solve should have not happened in the first place. By better planning, organising and communication, many of the issues would not occur.

Gaslight Manager; these are leaders who tend to manage a lot in secret, but make it seem like they are communicating the truth and have integrity. They tend to roll out new ideas and convince people that they are better off, even though they are obviously not. Gaslight managers use information which is incorrect to present data and/or points in debates. They often manipulate situations, which often make you question your sanity and your own facts.

7.2 Understanding Your Manager

Hopefully, from reading so far you should not want to be one of these managers, or work for one. It is really important to understand who your boss is, and how they want to work with you. It could be that you are part of a matrix organisation or a remote business. You need to take the time to understand what is important. To start with, understand what is important to them, what they want from you, and make sure there is a strong alignment. Joint alignment is the most important step to a successful relationship. These are the four key topics to discuss with your manager to help you to understand them, and set the scene for a great relationship.

Understand & Manage Expectations; from day one, you should understand what is actually expected of you. This should be documented and clear. Realistically, it should be referred back to during your structured meetings together. It could be targets, customer success or profit. Whatever it is, you have to get the bottom of what the expectations are, to make sure you can work on something. It's also critical you manage expectations; if something is totally unrealistic, it's better to say earlier than later.

Resource Expectations; you have to understand what is going to be available to you. This could include marketing budget, equipment, new headcount, accounts or stock. There are hundreds of examples. To be successful you will need resources, and understanding what is there for you is critical. Again, it is important to ask early on or flag any issues straight away if you need more of something.

How are they being measured; it is so important to understand your part in the big picture, and how your boss is being managed. For example, if your boss is being measured by profit and loss, you should try and understand this. Make their life easy by working to the same metric, or understand that their success will be your success. Try to see your job in the context of the whole business.

Communication & Structure; out of all the above, the most important is communication and structure. You need to understand how, when, and in what format they want to be spoken to. For example, is there going to be a weekly or monthly one-to-one? What needs to be covered? What do you need to prepare? When issues arise, when do they need to be brought in? Understand how, when, and why they want to be communicated with. You do not want to be an over fussy employee, but need to understand the points you should communicate.

7.3 Rules for Managing the Boss

Hopefully you have now understood what is expected of you, and how to work with your boss. So now, let's focus on the rules of managing the boss day to day.

Never 'Ambush'; a key way to annoy and disappoint your boss, is by ambushing them with information they do not know. Do not spring nasty surprises on them that they did not know about. They should never say, "Why didn't you tell me before?" Keep them well informed about any key issues that present themselves. It could just be to put it on their radar, but that is always better than them being surprised. It is also important that you do not tell them that you need an immediate decision on a problem, when you have just told them about it. They may have needed to prepare beforehand, and it could involve other departments. The same applies if you want the answer to a complex issue - give them the details well in advance.

Prepare and Be Accurate; before key meetings, prepare your case and information carefully. There is nothing worse than taking the time to have a one-to-one, and the person is not prepared or gives incorrect data. It means that the meeting was a total waste of time. Always present facts and evidence clearly; try and stay on schedule, brief and to the point. It is important that you respect and maximise time together as you are both busy.

Don't Be Negative & Find Solutions; do not complain about difficulties or issues. Be positive and bring solutions to events that are happening. If you have a problem that is beyond you, tell them in good time and work together to find a solution. You do not want to create a 'fire-fighting' relationship. The boss has a lot of problems, so try not to be one of them. Be the person who brings solutions.

Have an Opinion but be Open to Change; as a lead, it is important you be honest and open with your boss. Nobody wants yes people. If you have an opinion, new ideas or thoughts, you need to share them. You add value by doing so, but be open to all ideas. If the decision does not go your way, carry it out as though it were your own and show the boss respect.

The Emotional Offload; it happens... leadership can be desperately lonely. Sometimes the pressure mounts and darkness seems to circle. You naturally need to turn to your leader for that emotional offload. Emotional offloading allows you the chance to express yourself in a safe environment with no judgement. Always allow your leader to listen and validate your feelings. It is important to understand that everyone does this, and it shows your human side. You need to be aware of your boss's priorities, and that this does not happen too often.

The Boss At Home

The final step, and a very important one to understanding the boss, is making sure that you manage the boss at home. If you cannot manage the boss at home, you are going to find the one at work more difficult. The boss at home could be you, your partner, kids, family or friends. These are the people you feel accountable to in your personal life; their input and opinion is critical if you are to be successful. You have to be clear and make sure they understand the demands of the job role you are undertaking. This will of course, include your good and bad moods as a reaction to work situations. It is important to manage their expectations, as well as them understanding what a true position in leadership will take out of you.

Summary

- Avoid becoming a Mushroom, Seagull, Saviour or a Gaslight manager.
- Take the time to understand your manager, including how you are being measured, resources available, and their communication style.
- Understand and follow the rules of managing the boss.
- Manage the boss at home.

Chapter 8: Value & Due Diligence

"Don't ever allow yourself to feel trapped by your choices. Take a look at yourself. You are a unique person created for a specific purpose. Your gifts matter. Your story matters. Your dreams matter. You matter." Michael Oher

8.1 Personal Value

A key element of leadership is to understand the "personal value" or "personal stock" you or your people bring to a business. This is critical in how to negotiate your own package and self-worth. It is also important for you to understand this for your people.

But firstly, what is "personal value" or "personal stock"? These are based on what your career and experience is worth in the market today. Importantly, what you bring to an organisation. Value is determined on three factors. One, the demand for people with your skill set in today's or tomorrow's world. This includes the demand for you at your current place of work. Two, your actual resume and experience. Who have you worked for and how long did you spend there? What impact did you have? What were your results and success stories? Finally, your expectations from a company in regards to career and salary. Obviously, higher personal stock means you are a strong performer in a market with high demand. These three factors are important in creating your market value. For example, you can have a highly skilled professional in a market with high skills demand, but their career and salary expectations are too high. They may struggle to get the role they want. Another great example is if you are the top salesperson working for a company, your personal stock is very high, one hundred percent I would imagine. Once you have moved to a new company, your personal stock is back to zero.

Good people will only stay if their value is being met by their leader and employer. It is key that you recognise the difference and impact you make in the business. You will need to ensure that you are fairly compensated. We work in a time where loyalty is hard to come by and the market is very competitive for talent. Every employee seems to believe the grass is greener on the other side, and it is important to actually understand if it is. In fact, the average tenure has declined 25% over the last 8 years for employees. Of course, we work in a volatile and forever changing business world, but people in general are not as gritty as in previous generations. This creates the issue of what value you bring to yourself and your employer. You have to understand, a business will generally only invest in people they see hanging around long enough to get their return. This is why staying somewhere, building your reputation and career, is very important to increase your professional value.

Good businesses need stability to properly deliver value to their shareholders. Of all the leaders I have met over the last 11 years, they value longevity within a career as very important. In fact, along with actual performance, it is the number one thing they look for. Therefore, making good career choices and sticking with them is important. This is especially important if you want career growth, stock or equity in a business. Most stock plans and career frameworks are built over a three to five year period. This means that to be successful you need to be committed, and this will maximize the chances of a life changing windfall event. Remember, you need to have the track record and credibility to get the top jobs. This means it is important to choose where to work, and to make sure your value is met during that time.

8.2 Understanding Your Value

Here are five simple steps to understand your value-

Review your performance vs. people in the same position internally. In lots of managerial roles, there will be other people and peers at the same level as you. These could be in a different region, department or product, but it is good to understand where you fit next to them. Look at your performance and longevity vs. theirs. You will quickly start to understand who will get the next promotion or pay raise. It is important that you become the best of your peers to increase your value.

Review your performance vs. the market worth. Another good way to understand your worth is to review your experience in comparison to the wider market. This does not mean moving jobs to the first company that comes up and gives you a good pitch. It means qualifying the market more, speaking to recruiters where necessary, and researching other people at your level. I genuinely believe that you should know who your competition is, including companies and people. We all like to feel wanted, and you need to understand if your salary is correct to market conditions. If it is not, this does not mean you should immediately look for an exit strategy. Take the time to speak to your leader about it and work out what can be done. More on that later.

Ask people your value. Getting feedback from your peers and leaders is a very good way of sensing your value. They will understand how you are performing, or are viewed to be performing, so can provide some realistic feedback. Often, people believe their value is one thing, and it can be something else when given feedback.

Review career plans and set frameworks. Most good businesses should have career plans and frameworks that you can review. Naturally these will be reviewed during appraisals, but use these to ensure that you are achieving all the tasks that someone should be in your role. Take the time to understand your career pathway, and what the level above requires you to achieve.

Speak to your leader openly. It is extremely important that you have a very open dialogue with your leader about your career and personal values. They will have the most time and energy invested in you. Therefore, if you have questions, do not keep them to yourself. It is important that you share both data and your feedback with your leader. If you work for a great company and have a good leader but feel undervalued, it is much better to talk to them about it before jumping ship. Often, companies may already have something in their plan or it could have been an oversight. Be open and gauge their response.

8.3 How to Increase Your Personal Value

Naturally, you want as high a market value as possible within your career, and to make sure that you are showing clear signs of growth. Therefore, I suggest these four tips to make sure that you increase your personal value-

Longevity. As mentioned above good companies value longevity. But why? Longevity shows that you were a valued and consistent member of that team or business. Professionals who tend to move every few years tend to lack the long term discipline to make an impact and see things through. This does not mean that you have to work somewhere for ten years at a time, but three jobs every ten years is a good benchmark. Any more, and your stock could start to decrease.

Go above and beyond the job description. Do not get hung up on what is or is not your job. Always be willing to go above and beyond the call

of duty. Show your willingness to work hard to make the difference.

Make an Impact. It is so important and fun to be remembered. You want to make a positive difference where you work. Achieve something that has not happened before and produce something long lasting. Good people always have a positive impact in a business, just their presence and drive alone lifts everyone.

Be a top performer. We spoke about this a few chapters ago, but being a top performer naturally increases your personal stock. If there are one hundred people doing your job, and you are the best - of course, you are going to have a successful career.

8.4 Due Diligence

Conducting forensic research on a business and career opportunity, internally or externally, is critical. Too often, people just jump into career decisions without conducting any real research past interviewing. You can get swept up in the moment and flattered by all the great feedback. This can especially be the case if you are actively looking for a new role. It is very important that you see the opportunity in success and failure, but make sure you know what is behind the door before opening it. I would always review the source of information, but in addition you should consider the following points.

- **Business Performance;** take a look at the last 12 months performance of the business; sales, profit and retention. Consider future targets and measurements as well. What is expected in the next 12 months, and how realistic is it? It's critical to understand the context and why the results have been as they have. I would also suggest looking at the opportunity in broad terms. If the business has underperformed, it could be a huge chance to improve it and expectations could be low.

- **Culture;** understand the actual culture of the business. Not the one they tell you, but conduct some research yourself. Find current and past staff, see what they think, check their social media and platforms. See how long people have stayed in a similar role and what their background is. How many people are in the same role now, what does your internal competition look like and who are the teams you will work with every day?

- **References;** it is important to find some trusted references on the business. See if your future leader is open to providing references on themselves or the business. See if you know people who have worked for them. See if you can speak to a customer, current or lost. It's really important to see what people say when the door is closed.

- **Finance;** take the time to understand the financial situation of the company. Are they well-funded, profitable or making losses? The last thing you want to do is walk straight into a financial pressure cooker which you had nothing to do with. Take some time to understand the operating costs of the business or your sector/ region/ vertical/ business unit.

- **Capitalisation of Shares;** if you have a long term goal to gain shares in the business, you need to understand the shareholding. This could be at board level and at employee grant level. You may be part of an enterprise management incentive (in the UK), restricted stock options or just an options package. What are the total number of shares, the share price and plan for the business? Will you get a good return for your time and investment? Remember, share plans usually vest around four years. So you need to stay long enough to become fully vested and therefore have a higher chance of a successful exit.

- **Leadership Alignment;** if you are going to work for a business, understand the goals and culture of the leadership team. What are the actual plans and how fixed are they? Drive a close alignment between yourself and the senior leadership team.

8.5 Types of Companies

The way to understand a company is to look at how it behaves. When you look at a business, there are lots of smoke and mirrors. These could relate to their performance, culture and success. All companies want to provide a good image and boast about their achievements, as they should. Lots of what you read about companies is also true, as long as it is from a credible source. But you also need to be careful of taking data from failed or disgruntled employees, as their opinion will often be negative. The website 'Glassdoor' tends to be the mecca for either ultra-brainwashed positivity, or disgruntled employees.

We will now look at the main different type of companies.

- **Lifestyle Companies;** a lifestyle business is one that is geared towards supporting the owner's income and personal requirements, rather than maximizing revenue or growth. The goal of a lifestyle business is to create a sustainable and pleasant work balance for the shareholders. These are great companies to get your foot in the door if you can prove yourself. They are the type of business that you can add real value to, and you can become a shareholder yourself. The only risk is that these tend not to grow aggressively, and people with a super high drive tend to get bored or achieve all their goals quite quickly.

- **For Sale;** generally, these are businesses at the end of their lifetime and looking for an exit. You tend to sense the 'for sale' sign at the door when you arrive at the interview. These businesses generally tend to struggle to innovate or make high profit margins based on their current go to market model. They are often focused on making more profit through reducing costs, rather than making more sales. This means that they can be well organised and have policies rolled out across the business already.

- **Corporate;** some of the greatest companies on earth are large corporate enterprises such as HP, IBM, Cisco, ATOS, Deloitte or Ford. These are businesses that have great training, structure and benefits, and you can build your career with them for many years. There is a department for everything, so you focus on your task or position. They always acquire other businesses to innovate, and then integrate that into their solution offering. The only negatives are that they can be slow and very political. For some people, it can be a challenge to move from these to a start-up, where nothing is done for you.

- **Innovators;** these are businesses that are changing the way we do things every day. These would include businesses such as Apple, Tesla and Amazon. They are always established companies producing leading edge ideas and taking them to market. It is difficult to see the downside of working for these, but it can be difficult to get hired in the first place- to get noticed and get ahead.

- **Hyper Growth;** you may have seen these businesses called "unicorns". They are companies which have large rounds of venture capital funding, and grow way ahead of the revenue curve. There are many household name unicorns such as AirBnB, Spotify, TikTok, and Uber just in the App's world. These companies often do not focus on profit or costs but on scaling out the business. High pressure, high demand, and lots of fun to be a part of as long as the bubble does not burst.

- **True Start Up;** this is a business that is just starting or is a few years old, with everything to do. These businesses tend to be cost focused but also understand what needs to be spent. In general, they are very exciting to work for and if you want to, you can make a huge impact. But it is always a challenge. Often, you have to create awareness of the problem for the customer before you can solve it with the product or service.

Summary

- Understand what builds your personal value.
- Make sure that you maximise your personal value at work.
- Conduct relevant research and due diligence on important career decisions.
- Consider the different types of companies that would suit you and your career.

Chapter 9: Winning, Success & Happiness

"Earn your leadership every day."
Michael Jordan

"You have to expect things of yourself before you can do them." Michael Jordan

We've spoken about failure so far, but what about success? The reality of life is success and happiness can include moving goal posts, especially if you have a big appetite. When you tend to achieve an objective, a new one appears in your mind very quickly. Winning can feel like relief instead of joy. It shouldn't, but sometimes we want something so much that we can build huge amounts of pressure around it. So most success in life comes down to mind-set, and we decide what success is. So in this section, let's focus on winning, success and cultivating a happiness mind-set.

9.1 Winning Mentality (WM)

To have or to create a winning mentality is critical if you and your team are to achieve their goals. As we have discussed before, you do not win every time but you should win most times, and one win is nowhere near enough. What creates a WM is the ability to dig deep inside yourself and do whatever it takes to achieve the result. This could include extra effort, new actions or inspiring others around you in order to drive a different result. Winners understand that they must forgo instant gratification or pleasure to achieve their ultimate result. They understand winning takes time, effort and often, isn't fun. A winner's attitude consists of perseverance, humbleness, and a willingness to learn from mistakes. But most importantly, they are disciplined. Focus on these seven steps to achieve a winning mentality-

- Have clear goals and objectives.
- Do it and be consistent, even when it hurts.
- Make success an obsession and addiction.
- Relentlessly seek to improve.
- Take action every day to move the needle forward- little things make the big things happen.
- Move outside and through your comfort zone.
- A winner cannot stop, even if they want to.

9.2 Positive Mental Attitude (PMA)

You will have heard people say, "You are what you think." To build a successful team and achieve all of your potential, you need a positive mental attitude. This means positive thinking and having a strong mental mindset. Your emotional attitude must focus on the bright side, and you will begin to expect positive results. People with strong positive mental attitudes anticipate happiness, health and success. They believe that they can overcome any obstacle or difficulty. They tend to focus on the positive of a situation or event, instead of the negative. These are the seven steps to a positive mental attitude-

- Focus on the reality of the present situation, live in the real world.
- Use positive language and set positive expectations.
- Accept that things are not always perfect.
- Mix with positive people (removing negative people).
- Always look to contribute in a meaningful way.
- Take failure or setbacks as a chance to learn.
- Be grateful and happy with results.

9.3 Power of Expectation (PoE)

My personal favourite focus is the power of expectations. I personally believe that having expectations for your life, makes them happen. Those expectations need to live in your subconscious and control your life. Expectations create self-fulfilling prophecies. If you believe one day you will be successful, you will. The power of expectation sets standards, creates confidence and integrates goals into our DNA of thinking. Expectations can be powerful positives, but you can create negative expectations and disappointment can reduce expectations. It's important to catch the negative expectations and deal with them straight away. Your own positive expectations can fill you with energy and drive, whereas negative ones can lead to despair and despondency. The power of expectation modifies your thinking and behaviour for the better, or for worse. People with strong PoE expect to learn through failure and have a positive expectation of their life. Follow these seven steps to a PoE-

- Manifest what you want every day, plant the expectations and think about it like a habit.
- Clear yourself of self-limiting beliefs and block out the negative thoughts.
- Commit yourself to your expectations.

- Do not allow setbacks or disappointment to reduce your expectations.
- Listen to the little power voices in your life, telling you it is possible.
- Be positive & talk to others about your expectations- make them real.
- Reward the expectations being met when they are.

9.4 Emotionally Fit (EF)

We all know about physical fitness. How strong you are, how fast you are, how healthy you are. We have control of this, down to what we eat, drink and do physically. But what about becoming emotionally fit? The exact same principle applies. Being emotionally fit is the ability to handle situations, both positive and negative, in the right way, maintaining your focus on the ultimate goal. It is continually being aware of your emotional state and ensuring it is in sync with reality. For example, if you are about to take a risk, you will naturally feel anxiety and have a feeling of "what if this goes wrong?" Someone who is emotionally fit is able to focus on how to make things happen. EF is a state wherein the mind is capable of staying away from negative thoughts, or can process a negative thought into a positive. EF people are able to optimise a window of opportunity and understand how it can shape their future. To build a strong platform for EF, you need to understand that not everything is going to be perfect, and cope with disappointment. Follow the seven steps to become Emotionally Fit-

- Commit to regular exercise and a fitness plan.
- Commit to seeing friends & family regularly.
- Talk to yourself and others. Externalising your negative thoughts is the best way to defer them.
- Take time to recognise when you're angry and deal with it in a healthy way.
- Take accountability of your life, and take self-care and management seriously.
- Focus on the big picture regularly.
- Rest and renew. Take your mind off the grind.

9.5 Successful Culture (SC)

Within your team and business, you need a SC. A high-performance culture makes everyone accountable for a part of what it takes to win. There is a group expectation that the result will be positive. Great cultures accept failure as an essential element of the process of becoming successful. Teams tend to respond logically to failure and disappointment, with the intention to learn without blame. When change comes, because of the culture, the team is able to adapt and remain positive. The team is focused on hiring the best person for the job and building a pool of diversity. This means being open and accepting of new ideas in a safe environment, and focusing on winning. Here are seven tips for a Successful Culture-

- Ensure everyone has a purpose and it is recognised
- Communication is clear and often
- There is open feedback and mindfulness of others
- Embracing Diversity, people from different genders, age, religion and cultures
- Teamwork, people work together to solve problems for shared credit
- There is high engagement and loyalty from the team
- Everyone can see the growth and optimistic future

Summary

- Develop a winning mentality
- Have a positive mental attitude
- Focus on the power of expectations
- Improve your emotional fitness
- Create a successful culture in your team

Chapter 10: Reaching the Summit

"Never give up on a dream just because of the time
it will take to accomplish it. The time will pass
anyway." Earl Nightingale

To conclude your understanding of the leadership
flex, I want to focus on the twelve principles of
reaching the summit. The summit is to have
achieved your full personal potential as a leader.
Great leaders learn to use the cut and thrust of their
character. You can do this too, by making full use of
all the tools available to you. Your character is what
makes you who you are and what you are as a
leader. It's your leadership DNA, and the
ingredients in your personality that make you
successful.

In today's market, years of experience are
becoming less valuable vs. the impact one has in a
role, which is why you must always look to improve.
As a leader, you have to be emotionally aware and
always have context in your decision making. The
days of the black and white thinkers are long gone.
Staff do not want instructional based leadership.
They want to be led by dynamic individuals with
passion and emotional intelligence. Teams want
success through ownership and accountability.
Hyper successful leaders are able to tap into the

highest and best contributions of everyone. They bring a team together by unlocking the total strength, passion, capability, and spirit of each individual. Mastering this is all part of reaching the summit and becoming a great leader.

10.1 Own It

The first step to success, is that you have to understand that you need to be the star of your own show. You have to own it and take control of your life. There is always a close line between risk and regret. But it is much worse living with regret, than taking risks you believe in and owning them. Remember, no one is coming to save you and life is controlled by your decisions. The ability to own it, means you take total accountability for your actions and live life on your terms. You've got to be willing to work hard and act rather than wait. Drive the mind-set change that you are the captain of your fate, and expect the best from yourself. Finally, maintain integrity to your values systems, as this always steers our decisions.

10.2 Goals & Dreams

I am a believer that dreams are for when you are awake as well as asleep. To achieve your dreams, you need goals. Successful people always have goals, and a clear vision of what achievement of the goal will be like. They have clear milestones for progress, understand the obstacles that need to be overcome, and work every day to achieve their goals. It's important to focus on the journey that connects you to a clear vision; a target, an objective, or something that needs to happen to take your life forward and help you find fulfilment. Dreams should drive you and remind you why you're doing what you're doing. In your biggest loss, you should be able to hold onto your dreams to find your way back to the target. Make sure that you can hold yourself accountable, prioritise actions and define what you should be doing. However big or small, you've got to have dreams.

10.3 Think Big

You will never be able to climb and increase your skills if you cannot think at the level above you. This means that if you are a "Sales Manager," you should be thinking like a "Sales Director". You have to be able to focus on the bigger picture and think about tomorrow, not just today. Often, thinking at the level above you allows you to see things from a higher perspective, so that you can add greater value to the overall mission. This enables you to stretch your comfort zone, see things on a wider scope, and allows you to be prepared for the next step in your career.

10.4 The Master of What You Choose

It's so important that you become the master of your calling. Becoming excellent at something is so much better than being average at lots of things. If you choose to focus your career in a certain area, you should become obsessed with it and become an expert in your field. Study it, make it your absolute focus and drive. Make sure that you are open to learn and take on board new information all the time. Masters are obsessed with becoming number one, and understand it takes time to do so. This means patience and experience of failure. Masters want to understand every element of what they do. The average time to master something, is over 10,000 hours.

10.5 The Power of Courage

Courage is the ability to take risks and take action, even if you're uncertain about the future outcome. If you want to be a successful leader, you have to have an action orientation and be willing to take measured risks. Remember that great people are in a hurry to get great things done. They understand the importance of big action, and have a killer instinct. They have the willingness to do what needs to be done, whether they like it or not. It means being willing to take action to deal with a problem or unknown situation. How many things have you worried about that never happened? A key trait for success is having situational awareness and behavioural flexibility. Situational awareness is a full understanding of the predicament you are faced with, and the circumstances you are confronting. You need to adapt your behaviour in the best way possible to deal with the situation. Courage often relies on trusting your intuition and having the grit to see things through.

10.6 Find the Positives in People

A key aspect to climbing your peak is the ability to find the positives in any situation. Great leaders do not look to blame, but look to learn and build with people. Most people want to do a good job, and do not deliberately make mistakes. Leadership is about finding solutions and focusing on what happened when things have gone wrong. Being positive, means focusing on what can be learned and what can be improved in the future. Bad leaders are looking to find fault and blame. Positive leaders give praise, say thank you, and redirect people to do a better job. Always make sure that your team leaves the room happier than they came in.

10.7 Don't be Governed by Fear

Fear is one of the most powerful emotions. Fear closes us down and narrows our mind-set. This could be the fear of failure or the fear of success. What if you succeed and achieve all your dreams, then what will you have to complain about? Fear creates anger and frustration. Negative emotions and negative habit patterns are the biggest obstacles to success, and hold us back. We must stop justifying them. Don't take things personally, and stop the blame game. You are responsible for the way you talk to yourself and the results in your life. The inhibitive negative habit pattern develops from a fear of failure, when we say to ourselves 'I can't do it.' We need to speak to ourselves in a positive way and programme ourselves for success. We should say, 'I can and will do it.'

10.8 The Importance of Time

Everyone has the same time every day- no one has 25 hours. Once time is gone it's gone, the clock does not stop. Time is the one resource that is totally equal for everyone. You cannot store it or buy more. Your life is made up of the moments of time that we have each day. We need to make the most of each moment by learning from the past, planning for the future, but living in the now. Whatever you are doing in the present needs to be the best use of that time right now. When you need to get ahead, remember there are 7 days in a week, not 5. Ask yourself today, what is the best use of my time right now

10.9 Validation

One of the biggest battles we have is the search for validation, as we naturally need it to feel happy. Validation is the approval we seek and the natural comparison we have to others. This could be others in our chosen field, our families, or friends. Validation is often the process of checking out our ideas or making sure that we are doing the right thing. We thrive on positive validations. You must have met those people who ask one hundred people the same question, just to get one person to say the answer they want hear? To truly be successful, you have to be happy that you are making the right choices, so therefore feel validated yourself. Stop caring about what everyone else thinks all the time, and avoid the rush to prove yourself to others. Make choices based on what you want and what's in your control. A big step to success is understanding that two things prevent us from happiness. One, living in the past and allowing yesterday to affect today. Two, allowing others to influence our view of ourselves. What someone else thinks of us, does not mean we need to become or be that person.

10.10 Live in Reality

We all have our own map of the world which is unique to us and is our interpretation of reality. Everyone sees the world differently, through their own view of reality. Our job is to be as close to the real world as possible, and not have a misleading, idealistic view of reality. Make sure that you are asking good questions and looking for evidence to support your views. Staff will often tell you what you want to hear rather than the truth. They may often downplay an important issue, or mislead you with part of the picture.

It is easy to go along with this false picture and pretend all is well, but unfortunately, this can lead to making the wrong decisions or moving in the incorrect direction. It is very important as a leader to challenge assumptions and dig into what is really happening, so that you can make informed decisions and better judgments that make a difference.

10.11: Learn from Experience

Learning from life's experience is a key skill in becoming successful. Everyone makes mistakes and wrong turns. If you work hard enough, you will often be in the same place two or even three times in your life. But, draw on experiences and make sure that if you lose the first time, you can choose something different this time. Focus on finding the positive side of difficult situations when they occur. Life is full of rich experiences for us to learn from. The more we do, the more learning opportunities we have. We need to reflect on our experiences and use them to sharpen the sword.

10.12: Power of Mindfulness

Finally, an essential tool to be a successful leader is the power of mindfulness. This means having the empathy to read people and react appropriately. Never underestimate the power of listening and taking the time to understand other people's point of view. Great leaders have the power to tune into others' needs and concerns before they speak about it. They think of others and create win-win situations. Mindfulness powers the abundance mentality, and focuses on growing the cake for everyone. This means not just to hog everything for themselves. Never forget, lucky people create opportunities all around them. Often, because people want to work with them, and they have a sense of a joint opportunity. Always think of others and they will think of you, I promise.

Summary:

- Own it and take control.
- Make sure that you have goals and dreams.
- Think big.
- Become a master of what you choose.
- Have the power of courage.
- Find the positives in people.
- Do not be governed by fear.
- Understand the importance of time.
- Do not get lost looking for validation.
- Live in the real world.
- Learn from experience.
- Be mindful.

Conclusion: Build Your Own Narrative

To conclude, I want to focus on three key messages from this book. As a leader, you always need to focus on yourself and your team. Firstly, focus on your style and building your self-confidence. We have spoken a lot about great leaders and what makes them successful. I am a strong believer that great leaders are totally comfortable in their own skin. They are the same person in the boardroom, with their family, friends and customers. In times of success or crisis, they are able to make choices based on context and continually see the bigger picture. They become focused on owning who they are, and are ready to write their own story. It's famously said that true success is designing your life, then building it. The same applies for your leadership style. Always have goals and measure your impact. Review where you were a year ago, where you are now, and often review your impact.

Secondly, always think of others. Being emotionally intelligent and looking after your team is critical to great leadership. Trust and open communication are the foundation to this. Thinking of others does not mean that you are frozen, and can't ever make powerful decisions that lead to massive action. It means that when you make big choices, people are far more likely to come with you because they know you would have considered all options. It means that you look at situations with colour and real life context. It is not often that two situations are the same. Always consider the people affected. Through thinking of others, the relationship stays open and you are more likely to get to the truth. The reality of great leadership, is that you have to sell and sacrifice a lot.

Finally, remember that success in leadership and building a great team takes time. I believe that success and impact should always be judged over years. "Judge me in three years' time," should be the mind-set of any great leader. Often, when we see a successful person, we see them for who and where they are today. They are at the top of a mountain with a full trophy cabinet, successful highlight reel, and career fulfilment. We do not see the long slog, rejections, failure, people who let them down, studying, and all the wrong paths they took to get to the top. Lots of little actions gradually make big actions happen, and learning your craft will take time, commitment and discipline. Happiness and success are a state of mind. These can only be found through yourself.

Acknowledgements

Thanks for reading Climb Your Everest with Everyone, Leader and Management Handbook. I wanted to take the chance to thank the people in my life who made this book possible.

Firstly, Mentor Masters and Gary Lacey for supporting me publish the book. The work of speakers such as Tony Robbins, Jim Rohn and Les Brown whose words have inspired me throughout my career to date.

Secondly, teams and business partners for the last eleven years who continually supported my professional growth. Experiences are only great when you share them with great people.

Finally, my family and friends. My wife Fiona, parents for continually supporting my ideas and encouraging me to follow my dreams.

www.ingramcontent.com/pod-product-compliance
Lightning Source LLC
Chambersburg PA
CBHW070335220526

45467CB00001B/137